jane harris + jimmy edmonds

when words are not enough

creative
responses
to grief

QUICKTHORN

Foreword

'When Words Are Not Enough offers us all an insight into the power of creativity to shine light into the dark abyss of grief.'

This is a book about sorrow, yet it is brimming with hope. This is a book about loss, but it overflows with love and generosity. The community of bereaved people is as diverse as humanity itself, and this book is a gathering of their wisdom, guided and curated by the creative talents and parental grief of Jane Harris and Jimmy Edmonds.

I first met Jane and Jimmy at a showing of their film *A Love That Never Dies*, a remarkable work that documents their quest to understand more about parental grief. Their son Josh had been killed in a traffic accident in Vietnam at the age of 22 and the film starts with their own journey to Southeast Asia and the scene of Josh's death. The metaphor continues with a road trip across the United States, where they meet other bereaved parents and hear some remarkable stories of survival – stories that give voice to a fundamental truth – that grief is the form love takes when someone dies – something that radiates powerfully from every page of this book.

Jane and Jimmy had met each other at film school, so it was inevitable that their creative minds would filter their grief experience through the medium of film. *A Love That Never Dies* is but one of many creative journeys they have made to find new ways to live alongside their loss. In the weeks immediately following Joshua's death they had recorded the day long funeral celebration and made *Beyond Goodbye*, a 30-minute documentary that captures the rawness and disbelief of a community united by love of Josh and the value of honouring a life with a well-conceived ritual.

Now in this, their latest creative project, they have offered us a glimpse into the forever-different world of all who grieve. Beyond every funeral lies the rest of our lives. This is often when reality bites, and the immeasurable gap left in the lives of bereaved family and friends becomes a daily struggle. How do we live, who are left broken by our loss? *When Words Are Not Enough* is a foray into this chasm. Jane and Jimmy have continued to use their separate talents as psychotherapist (Jane), photographer (Jimmy), and filmmakers (both), to investigate numerous creative strategies that are firstly an attempt to find meaning again and then a way of placing their grief in a wider social context.

The authors' own discoveries are amplified by contributions from 13 fellow travellers all of whom have found their own creative response to their grief. As a collection it compels viewers to notice two recurring themes. One is the simple fact of human mortality. The insights contained here make us more fully aware that our own lives, and the lives of everyone we love, are temporary; and that finding the joy in the everyday is a precious and urgent task.

The other theme contained in these stories is that every attempt by bereaved people to express their grief in a way that is true to them starts with the sense of abandonment by friends and neighbours: that those who don't know what to say avoid saying anything, even sometimes avoiding the bereaved themselves. It is people who have known grief who step up. Both Jane and Jimmy describe the relief that comes from sharing their grief with an audience that understands – that their grief has been validated. Imagine a bereaved parent feeling that their grief for their dead child is not valid! Yet it is our awkwardness and reluctance to accompany bereaved people or invite them to speak of their loss that condemns them to a loneliness only they can understand.

In the pages of this book the bereaved speak loud and clear. These are voices that can help us all to overcome our fears. Jane and Jimmy have broadened their scope from their own experience of the death of a child and curated an intimate and poignant collection of stories that demonstrate their belief that grief is almost by definition a creative endeavour. Theirs is a proactive approach to grief that rests on a simple idea – that grief is about doing and making things to fill the void left by a loved one's death. The claim is that everything we do to ease the pain and accommodate loss, all those small (and perhaps daily) rituals we will inevitably perform to remember and honour our dead – these are all creative acts. Everything we make that acknowledges the way we have been changed by their death will be something new, something that wouldn't have existed had they not died.

Sharing the results of that labour is a generous act. Whether grieving ourselves or seeking to support others in their grief, the stories in these pages allow us to appreciate that there is nothing we can do or say that can ease the pain of grief. But that is not what we are required to do. Our role is simply to be willing to be present, to witness, to use the dead person's name and hold them in memory. A role that could be made even easier once we engage with the creative possibilities that grief presents.

When Words Are Not Enough offers us all an insight into the power of creativity to shine light into the dark abyss of grief. It captures the possibility of creating new ways of relating to those whose deaths we mourn and whose presence we yearn for. It provides practical and helpful insights, from grief theory to mindfulness, that can enable all of us to process our own grief and to become wiser, kinder companions to others who are grieving. This is a book to savour and to treasure.

Dr Kathryn Mannix

Contents

Joshua (left) with his parents on their last holiday together in New York January 2010

'*Saying goodbye is never easy,
but saying goodbye can also lead to
new discoveries.*'
From Beyond Goodbye, a film by
The Good Grief Project

Introduction

hen we received news
that our son Joshua had
been killed in a road
accident in South East
Asia, we were thrown into a state of utter
confusion and despair. Nothing had or could have
prepared us for such a calamity. We had
encountered death before – a father,
grandmothers, grandfathers, some friends and
distant relations – but nothing that came close to
the trauma we suffered that January day in 2011.
Our lives felt shattered. Time, if it had not stopped
completely, was now divided into the 'before' and
'after' of the most catastrophic event. How we
survived those early days of grief is still a mystery.
But survive we have, and the last eleven years
have shown us that human beings and bereaved
parents, in particular, have an extraordinary
ability to rise above the most horrendous, most
debilitating of circumstances.

Joshua's life and his death are scored into the very
fabric of our being – we will never forget what he
brought to our lives and we will never forget that
he died far, far too young, way before he had the
chance to fulfil so many dreams and to contribute
to society in ways that his emerging talent as
a video producer would have allowed him to.

Our grief has come with many lessons. Early on
we learned there are no rules by which grief would
play out, we learned to appreciate grief's many
vagaries, its massive ups and downs, its guilt-
ridden and angry moments, the way it could drop
you like a weight then haul you back even while
you resisted, back to the light of day. We learned,
too, that while we craved the exceptional nature
of our grief – no one could love Josh like we do and
no one can miss him like we do – we were not
alone. As much as we would want to hang on to
the pain of his absence (pain being that sure sign
he is not forgotten), we learned that many others
grieved for him too. Recognising the hurt of others

– his brother, his sister, his many friends – helped us to reach out and to share our attempts to regain some kind of normalcy, to regain a sense of purpose and meaning, to bring stability back to our lives, to accept his death and find a way of including it in everything we do.

We discovered that grief isn't all doom and gloom. It's not about sitting in a darkened room waiting for the sun to start shining again. Neither is it a passing phase, an ailment from which we would recover, and still less is it a statutory period of mourning. This may well be different for others, but we have found that our grief is not so much a process, or a journey (though it can be like that), more, it's like a condition, a state of being, something that we will live with for the remainder of our lives. We didn't choose it, but neither do we resent it; in fact, we have learned to embrace it.

We've now had eleven years of living without Josh. During that time we have come to realise that our

grief has been a series of creative acts. Accommodating his loss into our ongoing lives has been about finding various imaginative ways to fill the void left by his absence. In this sense everything we do to attend to our grief is about making something new, something that didn't exist and wouldn't have existed unless Josh had died.

For us, film and photography are the media we know best. In this book you will discover some of the photographic and documentary film ideas that Jimmy has explored as a filmmaker. As a psychotherapist, Jane has a deep understanding of the way our emotions work and how we report on those emotions. Together we share a curiosity about human behaviour and a desire to report on what we find. This drives us to make films. For us, there has been no better way of dealing with the aftermath of Josh's death. Photography is largely an individual pursuit – film production is a more collaborative endeavour. From the initial idea to the research, through to the filming and editing stages, and finally to screening to an audience, we are making connections – connections firstly with that club that no one wants to belong to, then to a wider bereavement community, and finally to a general public.

Both media can be a catalyst for new conversations, for the telling and for the listening. Throughout history people have needed to talk about their grief. Much in contemporary society tells us that grief is a depressing, morbid subject, so that breaking through the silence can be hard work, but along with many others who also grieve we have found that sharing our experience with the films we have made and the photos we have produced has been essential for our survival.

In the following pages we will explore some of these projects, along with what they have taught us. Also included here are the lessons learned from other contributors to the book, all of whom have made an intentional response to their grief, and have in various ways made the choice to share their grief publicly. While some are professionals, many have turned to the arts for the first time simply as a response to their trauma, but all have found that the process of creating something new to fill the void left by a loved one has been truly cathartic. In doing so they are not so much looking back to memories as re-presenting them in the context of their lives now. Gary Andrews' doodles are a daily account of his family's life now, even as his dead wife often appears to give him her blessing. Gillian Melling and Cassie Toulouse have taken their children's artworks as a basis for new creations. Sophie Pierce writes letters to her son in the first person – not from madness but as a need

to maintain a loving relationship with him, letting him know of new pleasures in her life. Sangeeta Mahajan has discovered a new art form that brings her peace, while Billie Oliver and Ruth Fitzmaurice relish the challenge of diving into cold waters as a way of connecting with their loved ones. These are all very different and uniquely creative responses to trauma following the death of a loved one. And in sharing their work – whether a photograph, a sketch, a song, a poem, a whole book – they are telling a story that can only be told by them and yet will be viewed, read or heard by many others.

This book is the result of much searching, of much trial and error, experiments to find a new way of grieving, a new way of living and being, of being active and doing stuff, and of trying to find a suitable, more equitable language through which to express our grief. We hope that you might find resonances with your grief and maybe some inspiration to tell your own story.

about the authors

Jane Harris is Josh's mum and a psychotherapist with a deep understanding of the way our emotions work and how we report on those emotions. Her empathy and her curiosity are key to helping others share their stories of grief, many of which have been included in the films they make. She is an accomplished public speaker and has appeared widely on TV, radio and the press.

Jimmy Edmonds is Josh's dad and a documentary film editor with many broadcast credits to his name, including the BAFTA award-winning

Chosen and *Breaking the Silence*, two films about surviving child sexual abuse. He is a lover of photography and a Churchill Fellow.

Together they have produced several films and photography projects, including *A Love that Never Dies*, a feature documentary that follows their journey across the USA to meet with other bereaved families. In 2017 they founded The Good Grief Project, a UK-based charity dedicated to an understanding of grief as an active and creative way of coming to terms with trauma and loss, especially that which follows the death of a child. An important part of this work is their Active Grief programme of weekend retreats, which supports other bereaved parents and siblings and helps them to find new and creative ways to express their grief.

what's in the blue boxes

Dotted throughout the book you will find our reflections on current theories about grief and some suggestions that we hope you will find useful on your own bereavement journey. These thoughts are the result of both our own experience, conversations with other bereaved people and extensive reading around the subject. We sum our ideas up in the *'ten things we have learned'* on pages 120–123 and recommend some books we have found particularly useful on page 126.

1
First steps: Jimmy Edmonds

Our Josh Is Dead.

Four words I announced at the start of the funeral – clear, precise, unambiguous, necessary. Necessary, because I am afraid. I am afraid of his death – I am afraid of my grief and of the life that now stretches out before me. I do not know now how I found the composure to utter these words, to face this truth so soon after he had died, and to announce it to the 300 or so people who had come to support us. But I did. And I'm glad I did.

I'm glad I respected our need for a direct honesty at a time when nothing else in the world mattered.

So now I hang on to these words – words that are the first lines of a new story. Stories are, of course, the most significant way of creating meaning in our lives, to make sense of the world and to share that understanding with others. In whatever form they take – be it through words, images or music, or even as a tattoo – they both help to record stuff that happens to us as well as allowing us to make things up, to put our own spin on those events.

Funeral for Joshua, photo top Fred Chance, above Briony Campbell

And because we are all compelled to tell stories (in ways and a language that others will recognise), they help foster connection, empathy and belonging. This last is especially important to the bereaved, who can often feel isolated and cut off from a world that has difficulty talking about 'morbid' subjects such as death and dying.

Constructing a narrative and telling a story is a creative act – you can tell it well or you can tell it badly. In telling it well, you will not only have communicated your purpose, you will have enabled the listener (or viewer) to connect with your emotions. Tell it badly and you not only lose the plot, you lose your audience and any motivation they have to empathise with your grief. I have learned this the hard way. I once told our story really badly in a lakeside conversation:

> *'How many children do you have?'*
> *'Three, one of whom is dead.' I replied.*
> *Stony silence.*

In the early days after Josh died, Jane also found herself telling the story badly to someone she

coping with grief | some theories

Is this normal? Am I going mad? Everyone thrown into grief will ask these questions at some point and will look for answers from those in the know. Here's a brief summary of contemporary theories about how people grieve that might help you understand your own bereavement journey. Always remember that these are models only, a useful set of tools that don't need to be followed rigidly. While there are common themes in the way we grieve, we all experience grief differently, and it's ok to dip in and out of different theories and find what works for you.

You might have heard of the Five Stages of Grief propounded by American psychiatrist Elisabeth Kübler-Ross in the late 1960s, formulated as denial, anger, bargaining, depression and acceptance. Subsequent grief theorists argued whether these stages represented stops on a linear timeline of grief or were merely tools to help us frame and identify what we might be feeling. Not everyone, they maintained, goes through all of them, or even in any particular order. The idea of acceptance, for instance, offers little hope to people facing a truly incomprehensible grief such as the death of a child. After Kübler-Ross died in 2004, her colleague David Kessler (himself a bereaved father) offered a sixth stage – 'finding meaning' – to include the realisation that our relationship with the deceased can continue after their death. This chimed both with the experience of the bereaved and with an alternative model for grief, *Four Tasks of Mourning*, proposed by William Worden in his book *Grief Counselling and Grief Therapy*, which provided a more action-oriented plan for the griever:

- To accept the reality of the loss;
- To process the pain of grief;
- To adjust to a world without the deceased;
- To find an enduring connection with the deceased in the midst of embarking on a new life.

This is a more proactive way of looking at grief but, like others, Worden emphasised that there is no reasonable time frame for someone to work through either stages or tasks. Some people might navigate them quickly, others might take months or years. That said, they do seem to suggest that in what became known as the 'grief work' model we must face the pain of our loss head-on. This is emotionally and physically exhausting, so a further theory, known as the Dual Process Model of Coping (developed by Margaret Stroebe and Henk Schut), argued that to 'avoid, deny or suppress' certain aspects of grief is not only normal but a healthy and important part of grieving. They suggest that 'grief work' and the idea of a 'healthy' grief is largely based on a Western, medical model that undervalues the more instrumental experience of grief (a so called more 'masculine' way of grieving) and instead relies on the intuitive grief experience (seen as more feminine) that is more expressive and willing to confront difficult emotions. They see grief as an oscillation between loss-oriented and restoration-oriented stressors that help us cope with our loss.

The point is that it's fine and normal to experience grief in doses – sometimes we can confront it directly, at other times we just simply need a break. It's ok to not be ok. Our grief won't necessarily shrink, but with time we can grow around it.

Funeral for Joshua, photo Fred Chance

bumped into on a visit back to London, who asked how Josh was doing. 'Just fine,' Jane replied. The thought of it still fills her with shame. Why the denial? Ask any bereaved parent in the early stages of grief and they will tell you that having to scoop someone else up when you break the shocking news of your child's death is just too much to cope with.

Telling the story of your grief is not easy. For us, in the early days of our trauma and raw grief that we were living through, finding the words was an almost impossible task. What else was there to say? Our Josh is dead – an open and shut case.

Keep it brief or risk facing a complicated and unsettling interaction.

This is why we need a funeral – a public ritual that brings perspective and a shared sense of belonging at a time when all seems lost. We had been to funerals before, of course. We knew the form – the entrance of the coffin, the eulogies, the specially chosen music, the tea and cakes, the hushed conversations – we'd been there, and we'd seen it represented in so many TV dramas, too. But we hadn't ever had to organise one ourselves. We had a choice, to go with convention or amend

13

it; to make it more personal, create our own version, our own account of the way we would say goodbye to Josh. To do this we needed a story for him, and for us, through a ceremony that would be memorable for the way it was told.

When someone dies you need to do three things:
1 **Legal** – you must register the death with the authorities.
2 **Practical** – you must dispose of the body, either with burial or cremation.
3 **Social** – have a funeral or hold a ritual or rite of some kind (or not, but that is a rite in itself).

In the United Kingdom and in most of the Western world, the disposal of the body has become entwined with the funeral. We have mixed up our need to publicly honour our loved one in a dignified and loving way with the moment when their body is lowered to the ground or disappears behind the curtain in the crematorium.

Many people get round this by organising a memorial service at some later date to celebrate that person's life, though the physical presence of the body is absent – they are not there. As its name suggests, it's about memories – it's about looking back to what was, to the loved one's life.

What, then, of our need to acknowledge our loss along with what the absence of loved ones means to us now and how we could begin to carry on without them? It was an instinctive reaction to our personal trauma that we wanted Josh's funeral to be disassociated from anything to do with the disposal of his body and for it to happen before he was taken to the crematorium. It seemed important that he had to be there, both in body and in spirit, so that our goodbyes could be attached to both his physical form as well as his memory.

I'm not sure that we realised it at the time, but the significance of creating our own funeral rite (unencumbered by the functional business of cremating his body) turned out to be a very important and influential first step in our bereavement. At a time of great distress, it seems natural to want to hand over the arrangements to the professionals, and if you feel you live and work within the safety of an established and reliable set of cultural traditions, then delegating is probably a wise move. But our own previous experience of funerals had led us to think that a half-hour slot at the crematorium with a service conducted by a stranger who neither knew us or Josh was the last thing we would want. If we'd gone down this route, I think we'd be forever lamenting our lack of vision... our grief for Josh might well have been overcome and complicated by the regret (even guilt) that we had not honoured his death as we honoured his life.

So just two weeks after receiving the news of our son's death, and before he was finally laid to rest, we constructed our own story – a drama in four parts – in which the audience played a role. Over 300 people crowded into a space normally reserved for wedding receptions. An aisle ran down the middle and Josh's coffin sat on trestles at the front. Honouring Joshua's life would fill a whole day; the next morning he would go to the crematorium.

But for now, he was with us and we with him. We didn't have to worry about the horror of his corpse being reduced to ash in an industrial incinerator – we could disassociate from that necessary procedure and concentrate on paying tribute to a spirit that had passed. And we did it in our time – not an allotted half-hour crematorium slot. We could take all the time we needed to remember Josh – the solemn moments with eulogies were followed by a celebration, with films and musical contributions, and then his casket was carried to a small, more private space for people to write a message on a ribbon, tie it to the casket, and say a more personal farewell.

building the casket | our first creative act

Scroll back a week and I'm at the timber merchants with Richard, a good friend. We are buying the necessaries to make a casket for Joshua's body – pine wood, architrave, dowel, Danish oil – no nails or screws. Richard is a quiet man, methodical, calm, an accomplished joiner and totally committed to helping us produce what is our very first creative act, something made from our own hands, something that didn't and wouldn't have existed before and unless Josh had died.

Over the next few days, we would be joined by other members of our community taking turns to help build this simple box – to sand, varnish and sand again – finding for themselves some comfort in a bond of friends all grieving, to a greater or lesser extent, not just for our son, more perhaps for us, his family. There's a connection here that is both physical and emotional. It's mostly silent work, for few or any of us have been here before, and knowing how to face this pain with dignity has not been part of our life lessons.

And this is a lesson, a lesson in doing and in creating something new. Perhaps the doing, its practicality, helps to ward off a fuller expression of grief along with the fear that I could at any moment dissolve into a mess of tears. But it has its purpose and it has its aesthetic, and once it's done we take pride not merely in the box itself, with its chamfered corners, its smooth finish and its rails for tying ribbons, but a new sense that the process of constructing something new (and doing it together) is as important as the finished product, which is destined to go with Josh into the incinerator and be no more.

The funeral event lasted well into the evening, and as his casket was carried off into the night we lit candles. We started with two main candles by his coffin and shared the flame, one to another, so that each had a small tealight cupped in their hands – an exercise symbolic of the way we would all carry Josh with us for the rest of our lives.

rituals

"Ritual is a practice that seeks to make the repressed visible... in ritual space, something inside of us shimmers, quickens and aligns itself with a larger, more vital element."
Francis Weller, *The Wild Edge of Sorrow: Rituals of Renewal and the Sacred Work of Grief*

For thousands of years, human beings have devised and performed ritual practices as a way of remembering and honouring their dead. Whatever the cultural background – religious or secular – there is (or was) a shared understanding of the importance of ritual in grief. The funeral – the traditional farewell – was the starting point and an opportunity for a community to support the bereaved, to honour a life and to help us all confront the reality of death, both in the particular and as an inevitability. In many cultures, communities regularly come together to take part in stylised and elaborate public rituals, not just to maintain a connection with the deceased but also to celebrate the continuity of generations past and present. Such is the Mexican tradition of Día de los Muertos, the Day of the Dead, a three-day, carnival-style festival that temporarily welcomes the dead back to the family. In Tanzania, in the burial traditions of the Nyakyusa people, participants dance and flirt with one another as they confront death with an affirmation of life. Closer to home, there's the Irish 'merrywake'– frowned upon by the Church for its roots in the pagan tradition – which calls for much drinking, storytelling, games and mischief-making, all part of the send-off and as a way of easing the suffering of the deceased family.

Grief and celebration may seem like strange bedfellows, but that's only because in the United Kingdom and throughout much of the Western world we have lost a fully human and meaningful perspective on our journey through life into death. As symbolic acts, funerals and other death rituals have mostly been consigned to a highly depersonalised funeral industry in which death and dead bodies have become institutionalised, hidden from public view, made sinister and feared.

And there's a cost. Without a communal sense of the need for ongoing rituals to honour and remember the dead, the bereaved are at risk of prolonged or complicated grief, post-traumatic stress disorder and other mental health problems. Crucially, without ritual – large or small, public or private – we are in danger of losing that essential and continuing personal bond we have with our loved one.

But our acts of remembrance need not be confined to that brief slot at the crematorium. If modern society has left us with few exemplars to memorialise our dead, we can create our own.

Funeral for Joshua, viral candle lighting, photos by Briony Campbell

You may have your own ideas about how to design significant acts to help you commemorate the deceased but these are some of the things we have done:

- We regularly light a candle in memory of Josh;
- We planted a tree on the farm where he used to meet his friends;.
- We hid a memory box under the tree and scattered his ashes around it;
- At his funeral we organised a 'viral' candle-lighting ceremony to symbolise the way his spirit is carried on in all our hearts;
- We have a playlist of our grief tracks. Music that Josh liked – and some he wouldn't!
- We take his photo with us at all times. Sometimes we rephotograph it in the places we visit to symbolise our continuing bond with him;
- We talk about him on social media – his Facebook page is still active, and there is a special site, named 'Postcards to Josh', for his friends to send messages from their travels.

These are just some of our own personal rituals that allow us to work through our grief in a safe and constructive way.

You might like to consider commemorating the life of your loved one by doing something that they could have appreciated. What were their hobbies and passions? Is there something you could turn into a ritual activity that honours what they cared about? Visit a favourite restaurant, repeat a walk they enjoyed. Even simple things, such as releasing balloons or writing their name in the sand have a way of helping us begin the process of creating meaning out of the tragedy.

If you are thinking of activities for a more structured and perhaps more public moment, especially on significant dates such as birthdays and death days, it's important to choose things that clearly mark the opening and closing of the event. If you are gathering with others for a commemorative occasion, lighting a candle, or ringing a chime or a bell will help you transition into a more contemplative frame of mind at the start and shift your consciousness back to the mundane at the end. Remember, this is your space and your time to express your grief in whatever form that may come. If you weep, if you smile, if you sit in the stillness or dance with abandon, it's ok to remain open and do whatever comes to you in the moment.

creative act number two | a film

Ten years on, would we remember the detail of that day?

Many people will feel a real sense of despair – an emotional low – once the funeral guests have departed. We relied heavily on friends, family and other members of our community to help organise the event. They have been there for us in many practical and supportive ways, but now they are gone – back to their own lives. And we are alone. This is grief at its most painful. For as much as the funeral was designed to make his death real, the reality has a long way to go before it can properly sink in. Josh's absence, as well as our farewell to him, still floats untethered in a memory bank that is for the moment too disordered to give us much comfort.

Did we anticipate this moment? Did we consciously or unconsciously foresee a grief that would be so foggy, so fuddled, so unforgiving with its lack of substance? Why else, then, did we decide to make a short film of his funeral? Was there something about having a record of the event that might give us a more secure entry into this place called grief? In this new world of ours where reality was constantly on the move, slipping and sliding, like a bee at the window refusing to settle, did we imagine that a filmed documentary would at least provide us with an anchor, a more stable ground from which we could reflect on the trauma that had created such havoc in our lives?

Beyond Goodbye became the title of our second creative act – a 30-minute video that is both an impression of the day and a testament to the healing power of the funeral we produced.

People will employ whatever creative skills they have to process their grief. When Joshua's childhood friend, singer-songwriter Jessica Carmody Nathan, heard about his death, she immediately penned and recorded a short piece that spoke to his passing in ways that only she could. A gift for us and a musical development for her. Others wrote poems, made slideshows, made cakes, told jokes.

We have our own skills – I have over 25 years' experience of editing and producing documentaries for television, and Jane is a psychotherapist. We could readily employ these talents to record, document and in a sense recreate a version of Joshua's funeral that in subsequent days, months and years would serve as a gateway to our memory of the event, giving substance to and yet again validating the feelings of the day, helping to make both his death and our grief real.

The process of making a film takes time; whatever is shot on the day needs to be catalogued, the best bits selected and assembled in an edit that could take weeks. This time proved to be a good thing, allowing us to slowly come to terms with the trauma of Josh's death.

Editing the film Beyond Goodbye

For us to create a meaningful documentary for others to enjoy, footage from the funeral needed to be supplemented with the testimonies and reflections of those who took part. This was also a good thing – we were learning how to converse with others about our grief.

Editing a film involves a very concentrated effort and meticulous attention to the detail of the contributors' testimonies – what to put in, what to leave out. Again, this was a good thing, as we were slowly discovering more perspectives and a more stable framework to understand so many conflicting emotions.

Grief and bereavement and the feelings associated with them are not part of any school curriculum. There isn't a readymade language for grief, especially grief that follows the death of a child. When a parent dies you are an orphan, when a partner dies, you are a widow or widower, when a child of yours dies... we have no words for this, unless perhaps it's the 'worst loss of all'.

Documentary films often turn out to become something much more than the original idea or purpose. This is true of many creative projects. Looking back at it now, we have a picture of a family in deep grief. At the time, the process of making it, of finding a way to express ours and others' responses to Josh's death, was cathartic, and a truly significant moment in our attempt to come to terms with his absence. Eleven years on, we can see how far we have travelled and how important it is that producing a record of our grief not only fills the void, it also enables us to share our story in a format that can be viewed by others, many of whom we will never meet. All this helps us heal.

2
Continuing bonds: Jimmy Edmonds

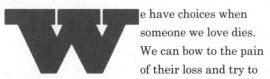e have choices when someone we love dies. We can bow to the pain of their loss and try to forget. We can tidy away their photos, their letters and drawings, put them in the attic along with the shoes and socks and the clothes they once wore. We can file all the memories and stories that these represent in a box called 'archive' and decide to move on. Or we can honour those stories, bring them into the light of day, recount them again and again, embellish them if necessary, embedding them securely into the narrative of the lives we live now.

For us, the cost of forgetting would be too hard to bear. We made Joshua and gave him life. We were his parents then and we are his parents now. We still love him as we love our other children. Our love has turned to grief and to deny it would be to deny the reality of his and our existence. It is, in fact, an essential part of who we have become, of who we are now.

'Our dog roams the other stones
while I sit on your bones
having a conversation with the air.'
Sharon Charde

In 1987, in Rome, an American student named Geoffrey Charde fell to his death from a wall above the river Tiber, late at night and with no witnesses. Since then his mother, the poet Sharon Charde, has been writing her way through all the dimensions of her son's death, penning her way back through a series of poems that combine a fearless examination of specific details with deep philosophical insights into the everyday proximity of death. In 2012, these were later adapted for a BBC radio play by Gregory Whitehead, *Four Trees Down from Ponte Sisto*.

We were on our way back from visiting Jane's parents in Scotland in the year after Josh's death when we heard it on the car radio. Potentially a distressing and perhaps a slightly dangerous thing to do while driving on one of Britain's busiest motorways, but we found it quite comforting to hear bereavement dramatised in a way that seemed to mirror so accurately much of what we had been going through since Josh died.

In letters to her dead son, Sharon asks him:
'Doesn't everyone die, doesn't everyone seek rapture and there is rapture really in these lamentations the untainted longing and the total clarity of the utter immaculate emptiness.'
After more than two decades, Charde wasn't ready to be finished with death. 'I wasn't ready not to find him everywhere.' She turns herself into several women: the one who shuffled the raw wild

❛*To alter the amnesia of our times, we must be willing to look into the face of the loss and keep it nearby. In this way, we may be able to honour the losses and live our lives as carriers of their unfinished stories. This is an ancient thought – how we tend the dead is as important as how we tend the living.*❜

Francis Weller, The Wild Edge of Sorrow: Rituals of Renewal and the Sacred Work of Grief

cards of loss, the one who was terrified to live with mercy and forgiveness, and the one who lived only to take care of her dead child. Like us, she would look for signs. Like us, she could hear her son's voice in the wind. Like us, her son dies every time a truck passes by too close. Like us, he walks across the room smiling at the butterfly that has landed on my wrist.

And now, like us, all those signs say the same thing. 'Mum, Dad,' they say, 'listen to me. I've led you this far; keep going.' And like us she talks to his ashes, and the flowers we planted around his tree, and to the crow that perched without any fear not one yard from us. 'Geoffrey,' she says. 'I want you to know something about your mother now. I have undone the padlock of your death.'

To unlock the padlock of Joshua's death is not to break the bond that exists between us. Rather, it is to enable us to look inside the burden of our grief, that darkened room, and to find within not just those memories and stories that were Josh's life, but our own history, too – what he meant to us and what we meant to him. When our son died, we were thrown into a state of confusion that perhaps only bereaved parents will recognise. However, in time – probably in the second year following his death – we came to understand that our grief was less a process or a journey with some kind of destination, more it was a state of being.

And rather than an historic weight trapping us in inertia and apathy, it became more like a whole landscape in which we were free to wander and discover what many others had found – that there are treasures in grief, or, as David Whyte observes in his poem *The Well of Grief*, 'small round coins thrown by those who wished for something else.'

In 2012 we were invited to read a Masters' thesis written by a local friend and psychotherapist, Fiona Rodman. Her paper, *Mourning and Transformation – Sifting for Gold*, explored the idea of change that is brought about by bereavement and which became one of the stimuli for the creation of our charity The Good Grief Project. There's that word again: creation. We were already hitting on the idea that we needed to create something new to fill the void left by Joshua's absence, that we needed to find some practical way of keeping him in our lives, of continuing that all-important bond that exists between parent and child. The following is an extract from the blog Jimmy wrote in response to Fiona's ideas in June 2012.

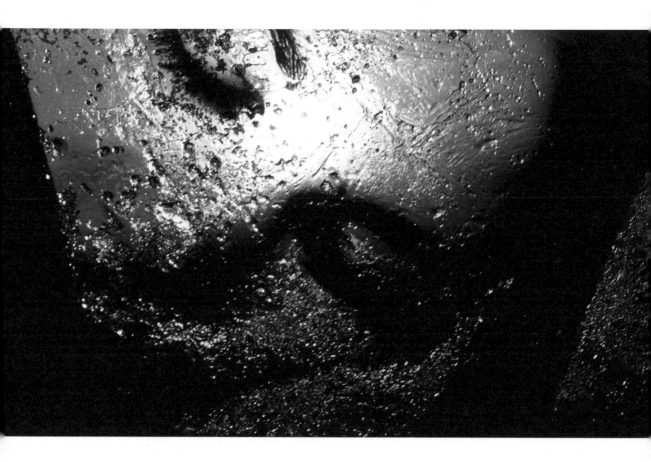

sifting for gold | a review

The drive to understand experience and make sense of the world is as vital as the need to breathe, to eat. And so it is that trying to understand and give meaning to life's final moment is equally significant. This might be an attempt to make sense of the inexplicable, but for the moment the process of coming to terms with and accepting Josh's death has inevitably raised the issue of our own mortality – the fear it holds and even the release it promises. A year and some months on from this tragedy, I am beginning to feel accustomed to my grief. It's not that life is any easier or that the pain of our loss is any less sharp, it's just that I know that pain better and my grief is no longer such a hostile companion.

To a certain extent I think we have been caught up by what we thought society expected of us in how we dealt with Josh's death: how to behave, what to say, what to feel. Even in this modern age, with its fast-changing moral and ethical codes, we are so influenced by longstanding attitudes to death and its aftermath that finding a way forward on this journey called grief is still limited by convention.

Sifting for Gold is concerned with the transformative power of grief. A person's death, particularly someone who is close to us and someone we love, is always a life-changing event. How that change is managed, or not, is the subject of Fiona Rodman's essay.

Her own mother passed away when she was in her early twenties, but it wasn't until many years later that Fiona discovered that she had not properly mourned her mother's death. At the time she had felt dislocated and adrift, that there were constraints on sharing her feelings with her immediate family. 'We were close,' she writes, 'as if clinging on to a shipwreck together. We could

‘*We don't learn to mourn at our mother's knee.*’

not, however, weep together, fall apart, sob and hold each other.' Her father, although loving and loyal, belonged to a generation that had known many war deaths; they were the survivors who had been severely traumatised by the horrors of war but who had learned to suppress open expressions of grief. 'Laugh,' he would say, 'and the world laughs with you; cry and you cry alone.' Fiona is only now aware of how this view had shaped her own emotional responses, leaving her feeling alone in a world where 'the role of tears as communication is completely denied'.

The standard model of grieving in twenty-first century Britain relies heavily on the stoic – our way of doing things has been to keep a lid on our emotions, to be strong and to weep only in private, avoiding any public display of frailty or despair.

The advice is to put a time frame on the business of processing loss and to find closure – after Josh died, a close friend even counselled that to avoid becoming excessively morbid we would eventually have to 'forget' Josh. The idea is that sooner or later we must 'move on' in order to regain the composure and the equilibrium necessary to continue with the rest of our lives. To do otherwise is to risk a pathological descent into melancholia and depression, and the social exclusion that will inevitably follow.

Death, of course, is all around us – over 10,000 people die every week in the United Kingdom, yet for most of us contact with death is relatively rare, and as individuals many lack the experience as well as the social models to help us deal with grief and those that mourn. And when death happens unexpectedly, many of us are understandably but

sadly ill-equipped to handle the emotions that ensue. 'We don't learn to mourn at our mother's knee,' observes Su Chard, the celebrant who conducted Josh's funeral in our film Beyond Goodbye. Conflicting feelings of sadness, despair, confusion, anger and guilt need to find expression, but if the emotional climate of society is such that we show only those emotions deemed appropriate for the occasion, then what will happen to the inner rage, the impulse to self-destruct and the high levels of anxiety, ambivalence or even the manic laughter that can overcome us from time to time?

Not being able to mourn her mother exposed Fiona to terrible and 'unlived emotional states'. Her experience of loss and separation were never really resolved but continued to provoke 'turbulent, unintegrated, long fingers of pain… that seemed to clamp my heart and block the flow of my being.'

I was faced with a similar 'block' when, aged 21 (a year younger than Josh was when he died), I too was involved in a road accident. This was 1971, and I was on holiday with my girlfriend in the former Yugoslavia when the car we were travelling in was hit by another, then ran off the road and fell into a deep and fast-flowing river. My girlfriend, Gillian, could not swim. She died. I survived.

I was totally unfamiliar with the feelings that emerged, particularly those of guilt and shame. Without the necessary understanding from friends or family, nor any professional help, I understand now that I too was unable to process my grief in a healthy way. Much of this was the isolation that I experienced. Returning to London after the trauma of that trip, I felt shunned by many of my friends, who had their own fears of how to behave,

24

openings not closures

'Mostly, we live in denial of grief, with the stupid word "closure" bandied round often.' This was musician Nick Cave following the death of his son Arthur, who died in 2015. Along with the 'babble' about other stages of grief – denial, anger, bargaining and acceptance – he saw these as so much torture, given that for too many people the idea of closure means leaving grief behind and 'putting the past in the past'. Sadly, it often reflects how other people would like us to move on in life, even to the extent of inviting us to deny our grief entirely. To this extent it's about their feelings, not ours. But it's also about historical mindsets to mourning with long-established cultural or religious customs that determine just how long one should grieve.

Mourning and grieving are not the same thing. We could see grief as the internalised psychological process unique to each individual, whereas mourning is the outward expression of that grief, represented in socially recognised and/or community-based funeral rites and traditions.

The truth is that we do not get over grief, there's no shutting the door and there's no tidy resolution or sense of a completed grief. There's a school of thought that instead of closure, the goal is to reconcile our grief and integrate it into the new reality of a life without the physical presence of our loved one, into our new normal. If this feels a little like acceptance, the question remains, how do we do this?

Rather than closure we see openings. Our loss and our grief, while painful, could be seen as an opportunity to open our hearts and our minds to new ways of seeing the world. Tragedy has taught us lessons we had no idea about before Joshua died. It may be that in sharing these insights in a proactive and creative way we can cut through the 'babble' that Nick Cave talks about – not only to help ourselves, but also to further an understanding of what it means to grieve in a society that often has so much difficulty talking about death, dying and bereavement.

By opening rather than closing the door to grief we have not only found a more authentic way to live, we can also welcome in those who are fearful, or at least hesitant, of accepting the flaws in their own lives.

as well as my parents' need to protect me from extremes of emotions. This left me completely disconnected both from Gillian and from my environment. At the time I would have seen this as distressing but inevitable, and my attempts to brave my way through it as honourable. To allow a tragedy such as this to mark me felt like failure, but I had been marked, I had been changed. And without the means – personally and socially –

to express my feelings, and with no understanding of the grieving journey, I became introspective, learning to cope on my own, actively avoiding close emotional involvement with anyone.

I lost contact with Gillian's family and to a degree I lost my way in life. Does surviving such untimely tragedies, or even the anticipated death of a loved one, have to be such a lonely experience?

a sense of self

In the years following her mother's death, Fiona identified a sense of an 'arrested capacity to mourn'. This led her to explore the cultural and psychological mores of our society that determine the way we grieve and how mourning has been understood by academics – as well as the bereaved themselves. Going all the way back to Freud, she discovered that after a death it is the way that we understand our sense of self in the world that plays a crucial role in our ability to regain the necessary psychological balance and the stability to continue living as functional human beings. Self, she posits, can be understood in two different ways – there is the idea of the 'objective separate mind' and the idea of the 'subjective interconnected mind'.

The first of these philosophical positions, the idea of the self as a separate finite entity, underscores a very Western view that we are unique and autonomous individuals existing alongside other individuals in a highly individualistic society. When it comes to processing trauma, of which grief and mourning come high on the list, our way of dealing with it is necessarily an internal and private journey of gradually loosening our attachment to our lost loved one until equilibrium is restored. It's a finite, even measurable process, which if unbounded becomes pathological – basically, you're sick if you grieve for too long.

Contrast this with more contemporary yet still relatively unfamiliar philosophical ideas that shift the emphasis away from the 'isolated' self and the separate mind to a more relationally embedded model of the self, in which mourning and recovery are seen as being facilitated or impeded more or less in response to and with the help of others.

attachment theory

When someone close to us dies we are often thrown back into a primitive state of mind in which our early childhood experience of detaching from our parents can be reactivated. How we respond and the way we grieve will be largely influenced by the way we responded to the effects of that early separation, often experienced as quite traumatic.

The psychological theory of attachment was first described in 1958 by John Bowlby, who hypothesised that the extreme behaviours that infants exhibit when physically separated from their parent (like screaming, kicking, clinging) were instinctual and evolutionary mechanisms designed to enhance our chances of survival. As we mature and form adult relationships, our ability to detach and reunite securely is largely influenced by the caregiving we received as a child. With a death, of course, there is no possibility of reuniting; our link to the attachment figure and the bonds of affection we have with them are irrevocably broken and no amount of kicking or screaming can bring them back. Add to this the fact that our internal relationship with ourselves is often based on the dynamic we have with significant others, then we can often experience a certain disintegration of our sense of self, of the wholeness of our being. Yet the attachment 'style' we have grown up with (Bowlby names four: secure,

avoidant, anxious and disorganised) will determine how we manage our grief and re-establish a sense of stability and security. Given that the child's success in her quest for independence is determined by a secure 'detachment' from the parent, it was perhaps inevitable that Bowlby's theory would come under close scrutiny by those who thought he advocated that mourning required an abrupt and complete detachment from the lost loved one. In fact, this was not his belief. Part of the process of adapting to a death involved ways to integrate the loved one – his or her legacy, memory and continued psychological presence – into one's own identity and plans for life.

Death and loss are a part of human existence, and we will all inevitably experience grief at some point in our lives. By understanding grief through the lens of attachment theory we can help the bereaved invest their emotional energy into building new relationships with those who care for them, alongside the continuing bond they have with the deceased.

Ultimately, the attachments we create with loved ones are infinite, lasting long after death: the bond is unbreakable. Our connection with the deceased may change, but it never really ends.

Searching out and recording the experiences of fellow travellers in grief, Fiona's findings were confirmed in two ways. First, while previous wisdom was to get over it and move on, these new ideas revealed mourning to be a two-fold process with a constant oscillation between deep sadness and attempts to reconstruct life. Now, as I write this, I believe I am in recovery mode. An hour ago, I was experiencing one of those painfully raw moments of missing Josh. Later, the hurt will return.

The second of Fiona's findings was that processing trauma is not best achieved in isolation. She writes, 'We need others deeply alongside us in our mourning, we need to be known.' Rather than a private, closed, exclusively personal experience, mourning is here seen as an inter-relational process in which dependency on others is vital for us to heal our fractured life, reassert our sense of self and our ongoing being.

It might seem obvious that to share one's loss and be supported by others can only be of value to the bereaved, but the actual process of mourning extends way beyond any public ritual in which an open (but limited) form of grieving is found acceptable. The funeral, that necessary rite of passage, has more often been seen as providing opportunity for a final farewell, part of finding closure rather than marking the start of a journey through grief.

Many people found that our funeral for Josh was not only deeply moving but also unique, with its emphasis on creating a symbolic journey in which we carried his casket into the main room at the Matara Centre, on to the next, then out into the night. But if it was remarkable, maybe that's only because in this country we seem to have lost the idea of a collectivised ritual and its ability to engage in, or invent, symbolic acts that give meaning to the loss that the community is feeling and to the possibilities for healing.

Fiona describes her visit to the Musée du Quai Branly, in Paris, as 'not like walking into a museum, but a prayer'. Displays of mourning rituals from all over the globe included ceremonial objects that marked death and its journey, seen as being important as much for the mourners as for the deceased. Items like the carved wooden boat inlaid with mother of pearl, in which the bones of the deceased were finally sent out to sea after the long community ritual.

What is significant here is the way a traditional community will come together and create elaborate rituals, in some cases lasting for years, in order not only to register the loss and its impact, but to help construct a voyage to a different relationship with the deceased. In the same way, in many traditional cultures, the dead remain as valuable spiritual guides for the living.

Our family was hugely supported by our local community in organising Josh's funeral, and their creative involvement deepens the sense of a shared loss while also providing the impetus for building a new relationship with Joshua. The viral candle-lighting ceremony was highly symbolic of the way we had all in some way been influenced by Josh and could share that with others.
Creating this ritualised journey, as old as time itself, and the healing possibilities that it holds for a communal sense of loss, is not so easy in a world where the individual, the lonely and the private self is the norm.

This brings us back to Fiona's definition of self, of how we see ourselves – our 'self'. Are we unique,

The person we were in their eyes

separate identities, or are we part of a continuum with the rest of humanity? In both cases, of course, we need to relate to others, but within the model that Fiona describes as the intrapsychic, or separated, self, we can survive without others in the belief that nothing of our own self has been lost. Not only that, but we endure the loss knowing that our mourning will be a finite process, with a final letting go signalling a healthy outcome to our grieving journey.

However, if our view of who we are is based on the idea of our 'selves' being part of a commonality of all human experience, a sense that we are all more alike than different, and that we exist as relational beings, then when someone close to us dies, we feel that death as a loss of part of our own 'self'. I suspect that all those who knew Josh, all those who had any kind of relationship with him, will accept that when he died something inside of them died as well.

A continuing relationship

If one approach to mourning is seen as 'a cutting off and a moving on', then the need to detach oneself from the deceased has obscured another aspect of the work of mourning – to repair the disruption to the relationship we had (have) with the deceased.

Rodman identifies this 'continuing relationship' with the deceased as key to regaining the confidence and the stability we need to carry on living, to carry on living with another's death. She draws on the ideas of psychoanalyst Darian Leader that 'we need to separate out the loss of the other from the loss of what we mean to them, the person that we were in their eyes'.

That last phrase: 'the person that we were in their eyes'. Eyes that no longer see; the person that we were and are no more. We lost Josh and what he meant to us, but we also lost that part of us that was Josh and what we meant to him. Fiona desperately misses being a daughter to her mother, 'of mattering to her,' and I have not only lost a son, I have lost my role as a father to that son. No longer can I advise and argue with him, no longer can I protect and admire him, no more long phone calls to gather up his news, no more am I his last port of call.

With Joshua's death we are changed, and as much as we need to come to terms with his, or any, death, we must acknowledge our changed selves – something I was not aware of when my girlfriend died all those years ago.

A year or so after Josh died, we joined The Compassionate Friends, a self-help group that supports parents who have lost their children. Jane will recall the words someone said to her as she entered the room: 'so who are you here to remember?' This would be the first of many meetings we would attend in which we were encouraged to name and speak of our child in a way that recognised and validated our grief as a shared, even collective experience.

'Through this shared space,' Fiona noted, 'a transformation is facilitated in which the child comes to occupy a different, still-living, inside space. The pain that the child is dead and will never again be present in the way that it was, is given room to be, but through a shared space and over time this other internal journey can take place.' As I read those lines, I wondered how this could be possible. In those early days following Josh's death, and with only memories and history to sustain us, with no actual Josh, I was confused about how a new living relationship could grow inside of me. Then I was reminded of the various creative acts that had helped us to continue our bond with Joshua – the tree planted on a farm where Josh and his friends would often gather, which has now become a focus for those same friends and family alike; the photographs I have made since he died; the film we produced as a celebration of his life; our new website. These all are sustenance for our new relationship with him, and they are all necessarily shared and communicative experiences. On Josh's still-active Facebook page we talk to him (Josh, we talk to YOU) and in speaking of Josh in these varied ways we acknowledge that new relationship, not only with him, but with each other.

Soon after joining the group we made a short promotional film for The Compassionate Friends. Titled 'Say Their Name' the video was another creative response not just to our own grief, but a

powerful engagement with other bereaved parents, all of whom testified to the value of speaking openly about their grief. As one contributor noted, grief is not about sitting alone and feeling dreadful in a darkened room, grief is about doing stuff, expressing stuff and being active. And because grief is about love and the unique relationship you have with the person who has died, to move forward it is important you find your own symbols and metaphors that tell of that grief. The thing that most expresses your grief must come from within.

That our ongoing lives have been transformed by Josh's death is beyond dispute. Fiona's conclusion is that it will be the deep inner work of reframing our 'self' in relation to others that will make them worthwhile once more. That this is hard work is

'I was confused about how a new living relationship could grow inside of me.'

also true, but we have also learned that in finding new and various creative ways of expressing our grief, we are continually reshaping and continuing the bond we have with our dead son.

The title of Fiona's essay comes from a line she found in one of Alice Walker's poems – 'now I understand that grief, emotionally speaking, is the same as gold…' Yes, there are special treasures to be found in our mourning, and grief can be good.

31

3
Running through grief: Jane Harris

'Jane makes no effort whatsoever – her inability to concentrate is a continual source for concern.'
School report for Games Deportment and Gymnastics,
Wellington School, 1969. Aged 13

I have never been a sporty person but in a bid to raise money for the Alzheimer's Society some friends persuaded me to sign up for the 2011 Bath half marathon. My dad, Gerry, was suffering from vascular dementia, and this seemed a good opportunity to honour him and help a few others, too. That was the plan, and we were well into our training when with just two months to go, Josh died. I had begun to get that wee bit fitter, a wee bit 'sportier', and had definitely begun to appreciate the difference I felt both in mind and body – more energy, more confidence, more love of life. With my son's death all this fell apart.

As I approached the start line in Bath I had a sense that it was all for nothing. I was numb, still in that early stage of shock and denial. The reality of Josh's death hadn't yet begun to sink in. My life and everything in it seemed pointless. I felt raw, thin-skinned, I couldn't sleep, I was having flashbacks, I had physical pains in my chest (stress cardiomyopathy – broken-heart syndrome is a real thing), and again I was experiencing that huge loss of self-belief.

Would the adrenaline of the moment keep me going for the half marathon? In the run-up to the event I had kept on running – more or less every day. Up and over the Cotswold hills, in and out of the Stroud Five Valleys where we lived, and along the canal path to the Daneway pub; 10 kilometres there and back.

Feelings can be simply ignored or swept away, and I knew that whatever was repressed always had a way of finding its way back, either through physical or psychological symptoms. It just wasn't going to be possible to go into denial or to skirt round the edges of this bomb that had gone off in the middle of our world. There was nothing to be gained from bottling up my grief... I was going to

have to find my way through it, a bit like Michael Rosen's book *We're Going on a Bear Hunt* that Josh loved me to read to him when he was a tiny boy: 'you can't go over it, you can't go under it, you can't go round it, you have to go through it.' This was raw pain, and I wasn't going to allow myself to pretend it was anything else. What I needed now was some form of physical relief.

So, I kept on running, even when I least wanted to.

As a therapist, I also knew how my own fears and anxieties were deeply rooted in my own childhood, and that in the aftermath of Josh's death I could get stuck. It would be so easy to revert to my old ways of existing. I had been brought up by a mother who suffered from chronic depression, and she'd gone missing so many times in my early childhood – which I later discovered was her being hospitalised. I was constantly told, 'Don't upset your mother, it will kill her'. Both my two brothers

(and me) had to tiptoe around as we learned to hide our own feelings for fear of the damage we might cause if she felt stressed or pressurised by us.

So, I kept on running. Feelings of 'I can't do this' were overtaken with 'I need to do this to survive.'

In time I began to feel the benefits – both physically and mentally. I quickly learned that when I least wanted to run was when it was most important to do so. Even those mornings when I woke to the reality of Josh's absence, I would put on my trainers and force myself out of the house and, guess what, I always found that however sluggish the run or short the distance, the effect was a real sense of relief and a huge sense of achievement… and release.

More than once I found myself shamefully sobbing in the middle of a field, miles from anywhere. I hoped no one would see me.

There is something about getting out in all weathers and the need to run through the pain that helped me re-evaluate my grief and see that this was my way of continuing my bond with Josh. Whenever I started out, I made sure that I had Josh's iPod with me, fully charged. It was one of the few precious possessions that had been repatriated with him from Vietnam. I loved listening to his music. It helped me find out more about him, things that I hadn't really taken on board when he was alive. One song in particular – 'Timshel' by Mumford & Sons, in which the line, '...death is at your doorstep... but it will not steal your substance' struck a hopeful chord. There was a message here that somehow spoke to the universal, that I was not alone in my grief, that perhaps my own experience was not that different from that of others and that if I dared share some of these innermost thoughts and feelings I could find a way that would help me be more authentic and less caught up in the shame and embarrassment of grief, of trying to get my grief 'right'.

I started to record some of my thoughts on my phone – sometimes on the run, mostly once I'd got back home. They're typically no more than three or four minutes – bite-sized tasters of what it meant to walk in a bereaved mother's shoes – which I then posted on our website and social media pages. The sound quality is surprisingly good. I don't suppose

I did more than a dozen over a period of a year, but looking back they chart the progress of my grief at a moment when I was beginning to be more comfortable talking about my love for Josh in public.

Much like a written diary, these thoughts helped me validate my grief and sharing them helped to normalise what had seemed like an impossible task – to see a future both with and without my son.

How we remember our child and keep them in our lives can take many forms, but we can make our grief more significant if we find some creative way of breaking through the barrier of privacy behind which many will shelter, sharing our thoughts for the benefit of others.

As for the Bath half marathon, I did complete it. With friends to help me I crossed the line in a time of 2 hours and 42 minutes.

In the next few years, I became a regular and confident public speaker. As part of my work for our charity I now give presentations on death, dying and bereavement at conferences and events up and down the country. I've even had a moment on BBC Radio 4's Woman's Hour.

I have found my voice in a world in which, sadly, there is still so much silence.

4
When words are all we have:
Jane Harris

> *The words dead and child should not be found in the same sentence.*
>
> Kim Garrison, contributor
> A Love that Never Dies

A mother's love:
Jane with Joshua aged 7

'There are no words... I looked at endless poems and searched inside my heart looking for the words that might describe our loss, but there are no words.'

These were the first words I spoke at Josh's funeral. I had looked through many poems and essays and found them wanting. It seemed there was nothing in the English language that could express the depths of grief we were suffering.

In those early days we were numb to any possibility of connecting with the universality of death, or with those who have, throughout history, written so many words on the subject. Our pain was unique: no one else could, or had the right, to describe it. No one loved Josh – loves Josh – as we do and no one could devise a linguistic formula that came anywhere near to expressing our grief for him. Perhaps we thought that to use commonplace expressions would somehow despoil the particular anguish we needed to feel as his mum and dad, as his family.

So, there were no words – then. Eleven years on, things have improved. We have emerged from that early dense fog of grief and have found ways to communicate some of our learnings, to connect with others who also grieve and discover a common language that binds us all, especially those who have suffered and known trauma and tragedy.

As we come back to the world, we also find that we cannot escape language. It forms us and we are formed by language, and not just by the language of words, written or spoken.

The title of this book is *When Words Are Not Enough*. That's because like our other contributors who have turned to the arts and crafts, we have found expression in the visual language of photography and film. This is how we connect and make life meaningful once again.

But that journey back into the world – from deep and isolating grief to a greater acceptance and willingness to share difficult thoughts and emotions – is one that took time and was done with great care. Finding the confidence and the words, images, metaphors to be able to connect has been a process.

When our son died we knew nothing of a better way to grieve. But, by joining with others (The Compassionate Friends, amongst others) whose children had also died, and by tapping into various bereavement networks we discovered that sharing our stories in a sense satisfied a deep human need to belong.

Feeling adrift and directionless in a world without our son we eventually did what our humanity led us to do – we joined with others who also felt isolated from a world that seemed so uncomfortable in our presence. Although I found my way to it quicker than Jimmy, we joined The Compassionate Friends and became part of the club that no one wants to belong to.

Sharing is a two-way process – it's about telling and it's about listening. We don't think you can properly share unless you do both. In a way, for us listening was, and still is, the easier task. Opening up about the pain of your grief by sharing the story of your child's death is to break the privacy, that deep emotional turmoil. If talking is difficult, we can find an alternative way of expressing grief, of telling the world what it's really like to lose a loved one, what the effects of trauma can be.

For us, finding the right words proved almost impossible. For others it's clearly a lot easier. Each to their own.

the language of grief

There is much about modern society and particularly in Western cultures that prevents us talking about grief in an open and inclusive way. As subject matters, death, dying and bereavement are seen as morbid and depressing, not part of the lexicon of positivity that seems to drive contemporary life.

You could say we have lost the ability to freely communicate our feelings of grief, that we lack a common language to express it. Unlike most of life's lessons, grief and mourning are not part of any school curriculum, so it's hardly surprising that death, dying and bereavement are such uncomfortable conversations for many of us to engage with. And it's not only at moments of deep crisis and intense trauma that we find ourselves lost for words. Many a griever will report well-meaning but cliché-ridden and frankly inappropriate use of language from those looking to support them. 'At least he's in a better place now,' or, 'everything happens for a reason,' or more commonly, 'I'm sorry for your loss,' as if you had mislaid a child in the supermarket.

The result is a kind of invisible barrier between the bereaved and the rest of society. It's a lonely place to be at a time in your life when you need the empathy and compassion of others more than ever.

So, language matters. It is critical to every griever that we all find a more appropriate way of conveying what are actually universal feelings of pain, sadness, confusion and insecurity that are all part of the grieving process. The language of grief, like the language of love, can take many forms. It's not confined to the literally word-bound. Our own discovery is that all art forms – music, photography, painting, knitting, writing, even physical exercise – and a simple engagement with nature are perfectly adequate and appropriate ways of communicating your experience of grief.

Whatever works for you is what is important, given that language is how we find meaning and purpose again at a time in our lives when all seems broken and worthless.

5
Letters to a son: Sophie Pierce

In 2017, Sophie Pierce's 20-year-old son Felix died suddenly and unexpectedly. She has found that both writing and outdoor swimming have helped her in the aftermath of this devastating loss.

Today I went to see your grave again. As always seems to be the case when I visit, the weather was quite volatile, with big clouds moving around but bright sunshine also. There were two gravediggers busily working away. One with a small digger and another manually marking out a new grave and digging away the topsoil by hand. I stopped to chat with him and he explained how he used to dig all the graves completely by hand but the ground is so full of rocks he was starting to hurt his back. He asked why I was there and I explained that I was coming to visit you. He said how sorry he was and I felt quite tearful.

It's now several years since Felix died, and yet still, frequently, I am taken over by an alienating sense of disbelief and absurdity. I can be walking along the street, or sitting at my desk, and I am suddenly gripped by a sense of unreality, and also sometimes, fear. How can this have happened? How can he have died? It barely seems possible.

If you've experienced the sudden and unexpected death of a loved one, this is one of the most profound changes in your life you have to deal with. A continuing sense of disbelief, a kind of dissonance between the reality of life post the loss,

and the way life is supposed to turn out. And this is accentuated by the fact that life continues on in the same vein for most people around you, while for you, life is catastrophically altered. So, on many levels, you feel out of synch with the normal world.

I have found that tackling this altered state head-on, by writing, has helped. It has helped Felix's death feel more real. It is a way of actively engaging with the incomprehensible fact that he is dead, which gives me a feeling of greater connection with what has happened. This in turn helps me to live slightly more easily with it.

Two months have gone by and your headstone is not yet in place. It was ordered ages ago. All the headstones are the same; these are the rules. A rectangular piece of slate with the name and the dates, carved by the same stonemason. I want the marker to be there. I want your name to be in place. This is very important to me.

Felix was a gentle, beautiful young man who was just starting out in life. A student at the University of Leicester, he was found dead in his room after not turning up for lectures for a couple of days. I was the one who raised the alarm and arrived moments after paramedics had forced their way into his room and found him dead inside. Instantly,

Sophie Pierce with her son Felix,
photo Alex Murdin

Very soon, though, I found myself writing letters to Felix. It was a way of dealing with the shock. I was kind of pretending he was still there. Which of course, in a way, he was, and he still is, because he will always be my son, whether he is dead or alive. I wanted to talk to him, I wanted to keep open that channel of communication, I wanted to express my thoughts, my grief, my anger, my disbelief, my rage and my utter devastation at his death.

The wind dropped and the sun came out and I lay down by your grave and shut my eyes. The sun was really quite hot on my face. I could hear lambs bleating and the odd seagull, and I thought of your body beside me, underground, decaying. It's now over two months since you died. I wondered if your skin is still intact. Or has it disappeared?

Weeks and months went by, and I continued to write to him. The notebook in which I wrote the letters became a safe space where I could explore my feelings and what was happening to me. Writing about my pain helped to dissipate it and to give me perspective. It didn't solve anything, but it was a way of getting through each day.

All the while the two gravediggers were chatting to each other about this and that, how one had a leak in his radiator, the relative merits of the different engine sizes of Discovery 4 x 4s. Then

‘*Life continues on in the same vein for most people around you, while for you, life is catastrophically altered.*’

my life, and that of my family, changed forever. Felix died from SUDEP – sudden unexpected death in epilepsy. It is not known why SUDEP happens, but it turns out Felix was in a high-risk group, being young and male. The whole thing felt utterly senseless, here was a normal and, apart from his epilepsy, fit young man, his life cut short.

Those first days after he died were surreal. I remember the evening I got back from Leicester, the day after the shocking discovery that he was dead. We sat watching Crufts on the TV in a kind of stunned daze. Friends came round with food and flowers. I don't remember a lot of the detail of those initial few days.

> *When I am in the water I am paused in a liminal space. It mirrors the strange world I find myself in, after Felix's death.*

they started the digger up and soon had a vast mound of soil, some
of which they removed. So, it wasn't exactly a contemplative visit to you this time, but in a funny way it was quite nice they were there doing their work, the cycle continues.

It also helped me deal with the fact that the unthinkable had happened. As someone who is suddenly and unexpectedly bereaved, you are constantly asking yourself the question, why? To which, of course, there is no answer, and there never will be any answers. But simply writing down the word 'why', articulating that question to myself, and seeing it in black and white on the page, was somehow helpful. Yes, the unthinkable had happened, and here I was writing about it. It somehow made it more real, and also, in an odd way, more valid.

I also found consolation in the natural world. I was already an outdoorsy person before Felix died, but since his death the landscape and countryside around me have become even more important to me. In particular, I have found that swimming outdoors, immersing myself in the sea, rivers and lakes, has helped.

Afterwards I drove down to North Quay and had a delicious swim despite the fact that the water was

pretty brown from all the rain.
It was warm, and I swam upstream to where I could see the burial field and blew you a kiss. I swam from one side of the river to the other, and then moved along close to the bank with its overhanging trees. I saw something white on the surface ahead. As I got closer, I could see that it was a pristine white feather, curled up at each end like a small boat floating along. Then a beautiful wooden sailing boat passed me, a big one with a cabin, powered just by the wind, the sails cracking as the boat moved by. Then, up from Dartmouth, came a motorboat, and after that a group of seven red and turquoise traditional open canoes with some loud teenagers on board. All the time I quietly observed from my position under the trees, hidden as the boats went by, just moving gently around in the water for no other reason than that I like the feeling of being suspended there, in time and place, paused.

When I am in the water I am paused in a liminal space. It mirrors the strange world I find myself in, after Felix's death. Physically, the cold water sends my body into a sharp response, like a re-set button, and this is somehow helpful. In the water, I am connecting with the elements, with life itself, in an unmediated way. The first Christmas after Felix died, I had a profound experience swimming in the wintery-cold waters of the River Dart. As

Sophie taking a dip on Dartmoor, photo Dan Bolt

the cold gripped my body, I felt a deep connection back to Felix, to when he was a seed inside me, I felt we were somehow together again, that he was present. The feeling was wordless, primitive, elemental. I think this is connected to the fact that his body is gone and buried, he has returned to the earth, he is part of the earth and the elements. It comes back to that phrase from the Bible: 'dust thou art and unto dust shalt thou return'.

Now I am writing a book incorporating my letters to Felix and my experiences in the aftermath of his death, and this, too, is a positive thing. I hope my story will help others, but, more importantly for me, I am creating something beautiful out of his death, and also something that will be a permanent memorial to him. It will keep his name alive.

The Green Hill: Letters to a Son, by Sophie Pierce, will be published by Unbound, 2023.

The charity SUDEP Action provides support to families whose loved ones die of SUDEP. Find out more at sudep.org

6
Impossible words: Jo Bousfield

Jo Bousfield has worked in theatre as an actor, director and writer for over 40 years. She has a particular interest in working with young people and community. Her 31-year-old daughter Harrie died in 2012 of spinal cancer.

Jo Bousfield with her daughter Harrie

I have always been someone who finds solace in the company of people. The sharing of my feelings with friends, family and counsellors supported me a lot through my daughter's illness, treatment, terminal diagnosis and death. The sharing continues in my life after her death and will ever be so! But sometimes people aren't available, or it feels inappropriate to bring up my grief, so I talk to myself, chatting it through in my head, or by scribbling thoughts in my notebook. I love the written word, the power and shape of text, the world of language that has evolved over the past 200,000 years. 'Letting it out' on paper (or on a device) is cathartic, and that helps. As a seasoned writer, if I then edit and hone some words I have written, I have the satisfaction of seeing my feelings 'displayed' in front of me and can reflect a bit more on this extraordinary thing that has happened to me, and live with it, as the believable in unbelievable circumstances. Because, of course, how on earth can this have happened to ME? Other people have tragedies, not me, other people have a child who dies, not me.

I was asked to be involved in a local arts project whereby I was given a random grid reference from the land around my town. I was to visit that place on the local map and create a piece of writing about it. When I looked at the grid reference, I realised that it was the exact spot where, in the four days leading up to my daughter's operation (when a surgeon would attempt to remove the tumour from her spinal cord) she and I had walked, to watch the sun go down. Those were the last four days that she was able to use her legs, from then on, she was a wheelchair user, paralysed from the waist down.

I wrote this poem for the art project:

X marks the spot
My love and I did go
Against the odds

Perched on the slope
Sharing altitude
Preparing for change

Look out Look out Look out

Surrounded with falling
Still in the breathing
Body of landscape

Our soft spot
In a
Fistful of valleys

I read that again and feel desolate, shocked and tearful. Strong feelings. But I don't want to avoid feeling. Feeling is real. Feeling is being alive. Death takes away our loved ones. But that doesn't mean that we can't live well, however impossible that is at first.

Below: Jo Bousfield with photo of her daughter Harrie

7
Reframing grief: Jimmy Edmonds

Diary entry Wednesday 4th May, Cumbria.

And I pass on climbing an easy slope by the side of the stream looking for a moment where I make another story of paper and running water.

Nothing moves under the soft brush of wind.

Josh, be with me, let us step across, under the tree with its dangling roots, past last year's bracken, and climb to that spot – level with new grass where I can unload the day pack, place a camera in the shade and study the falls. There are small pools here, miniature beaches, and the constant rush of white water, bubbling, splashing refusing to stop – forever the water runs down the hillside carving a way through time, unconcerned with the past or the future.

I've lined up one shot, but I want a long exposure to blur the running water, so I balance the camera on a pile of stones – it takes forever, and I wonder if it's worth it. The sun is on my back as I crouch right down to get a view through the viewfinder. We are taking our time to get it just right. I want it to be right – you must be exactly square on in the frame – you have now become my photo, no longer Josh, but my photo in my photo.

And it feels like I'm losing you to a picture.

It's May 2011. Four months have passed since Josh died. I had taken a short break with some friends to Wasdale, in the Lake District. While

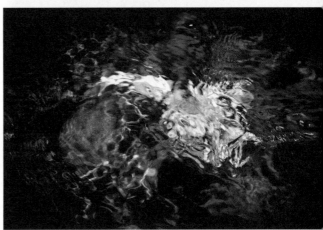

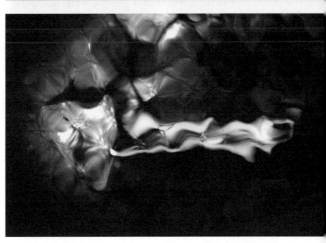

Nothing lasts forever

they enjoyed being together in this glorious landscape, I had taken off on my own. I carry a camera with me all the time, in the same way that I now carry Josh with me all the time and his business card, too. He had had them made using the photo I had taken of him with his eyes closed, so there's a deep connection between us – between me and my passion, and Josh and his work as a video producer. 'Joshed' it says on the front – short for Josh Edmonds. You've been 'Joshed' was what happened when you worked with him.

My fear, even in these early days of grief, was that I would forget him. This is probably a common fear and although I didn't think it at the time, it's probably quite normal to invent strategies to make sure you don't forget, to stay in touch with everything that he was, the sound of his voice, the flow of his hair, his smell, his dry laugh, the sardonic look he gave you if he sensed you getting stressed… yes, all the lovable and perhaps not so lovable bits of him that we need to prevent disappearing. This photograph, this business card proved to be an excellent memento and very handy when it came to one of my first attempts to create some kind of small ongoing ritual to process my grief.

I do not believe in an afterlife so I felt a little foolish when I started leaving Josh's business cards in places possibly where others might find them, but mostly in landscapes that we would both enjoy. Stuck on a gatepost up a farm track or wedged into a rock face looking down the valley, anywhere where there was an immediate connection with

nature, where it would be at the mercy of the elements; and in time would weather and fade. I was wondering whether knowing that his card would decompose, I would better come to terms with the reality of his death, that as his image faded, I would then perhaps be more able to let him go. It felt like it was going to be a long time before I could accept the idea of his being dead, before I could see his death as more commonplace;

Left: Image by Stefan Keller. Right: Photo by Dan Chung

before I was prepared to see him take his place in the shared anonymity of all the world's dead.

This is where the need to photograph his cards in these chosen landscapes came in. To photograph is to preserve, to make a potentially indestructible record of a moment in time, to keep our memories safe. But in making further photographs of Josh's photograph, was I trying to allay that deep anxiety that nothing lasts forever, when a photograph is in itself evidence that time has moved on?

On returning home from Cumbria, I started trying to put these ideas into some kind of context. Nothing of what we were doing, to find some kind of creative response to our grief, was out of the ordinary. Photography especially is recognised as a valuable tool for coping with grief, not just as a source of memory but with a long history of representing death and mourning in many different ways.

I began by looking for some good examples of what others had done in this area and found that Josh's sister Rosa had already explored the subject as part of her first year art course. In one essay, *Making it Real – Death and Photography*, she'd posed some very challenging questions – how far, she asks, is the act of taking someone's photograph a subconscious attempt to protect ourselves for when that person dies?

As we have noted, every photo we take will likely outlive its subject and as such has enormous potential to transcend that final moment between life and death, a fact well recognised by artists and photographers ever since the medium was discovered 200 years ago. But by googling a combination of various words – grief, photography, death, bereavement – I found little that spoke to my own experience of life since Josh died. Beautiful photographs as they are, mostly they seem to fall into high art or reportage, neither of which seem to be of much use to anyone looking to express their own very personal feelings in the days, months and years following the death of a child.

Typical would be this photo of grieving parents following an earthquake in China (see above right). Although as a press photo it has the potential for a sort of anonymous association for the viewer (we can feel their pain), it does little, I suspect, to help the mum and dad who have just lost their daughter. Why? Well, I think it's because they haven't been involved in the real work of taking the photograph. Did they know the photograph was being taken or did they pose suitably grief-stricken in the rubble, their daughter's image conveniently arranged so that the world can see her in full view? This is an image of tragedy for public consumption and feeds a very commonplace idea of what grief should look like but, buried as it is in the historicity of the moment, can it ever convey what grief really feels

Image courtesy of Now I Lay Me Down to Sleep

'*... but maybe the tears are necessary and maybe they feed the creative process.*'

Feedback from a workshop participant

like as one of life's longest-lasting experiences?

Now I Lay Me Down to Sleep (NILMDTS) is a sort of photo agency that will record for you a moment with your child who has died at birth. This is a free, professional service in the tradition of post-mortem photography that was popular in the United States at the end of the nineteenth century, when child death in the family was commonplace, though we can assume no less traumatising.

Now, as then, these photographs carry a huge emotional charge both for the bereaved families and for us strangers looking on. Unlike a press photograph, they demand the active participation of the sitters. A mother has taken her dead baby in her arms and posed specifically for the camera.

She is performing a drama with the shortest of stories, but one that will have lasting impact and as such has the potential for huge therapeutic effect. The moment is real, both physically and emotionally. She is taking the first step in a life's work of continuing her bond with her child. This is a lasting image that has captured a hugely significant moment, and one in which she can return to time and again as she remembers and tries to construct what (or who) might have been.

It was with these thoughts in mind that Jane and I started to consider how photography can help us to grieve better. As we developed our practice, we realised that others could benefit, too, so that in turn we began offering photography workshops to a number of bereavement support networks.

'Every photograph I make now helps to liberate the pain of our grief from the past.'

a mindful grief

Mindfulness is a good way to ground oneself in the midst of powerful, potentially overwhelming emotions that exhaust both the mind and the body, especially those that will come with grief. It's been practised for centuries and can be described as bringing one's attention in a particular way to the present experience on a moment-to-moment basis, without judgement yet with a curious attitude.

It is natural for humans to try to avoid pain and suffering. We don't want to hurt, but realistically, grief is part of the human experience. Mindfulness is not designed to minimise that pain or to convince people that everything is ok, but rather to help you recognise the reality of your circumstances, and to do so in a self-aware and self-compassionate way.

You don't need to be a Buddhist to be 'mindful', but the practice is deeply connected to the Buddhist concept of impermanence. When someone sees only permanence, they may look to the future obsessively or dwell too much on the past. However, when we accept impermanence, that the world is in constant movement and change, we can better appreciate each and every moment as being different and allow ourselves to stay focused on the present moment – from moment to moment.

This can be very useful when dealing with our grief. Both mindfulness and the concept of impermanence remind us that pain and sorrow, like everything else, are temporary experiences. Does this mean grief goes away completely? Of course not. But with practice we will come to recognise how our grief fluctuates from day to day, how it ebbs and flows, how it changes shape sometimes by the hour – from moment to moment.

Mindfulness is not mindlessness, neither is it the same as avoidance. In fact, mindfulness can make us much more aware of the specific thoughts and feelings that are consuming us right now – in this specific moment. There are two common ways by which many of us cope with grief. Either by being consumed by our suffering or disavowing it. Neither are particularly helpful – all of the time. In the ups and downs of grief, mindfulness can help reduce the extremes so that when grief seems relentless, we can acknowledge it isn't permanent.

Mindfulness can be done anywhere and at any time. Find a place to sit still with eyes closed or lowered, or walk with concentration. Focus attention to different parts of your body, but especially your breath, noticing the rise and fall of your chest and the feel of the air in your nostrils – your mind will occasionally wander to the chitchat of thoughts of other things in your life – this is normal – you just need to bring your attention gently and without blame back to the breath.

Mindful walking can be particularly helpful when we are distracted and concentration eludes us. Attention to the micro movement can offer respite when all else fails. It's not about success or failure, it's about simply trying it out.

Practising mindfulness can become a way of life in which we develop an awareness of the present – our thoughts and feelings, our physical experience, and the world around us as they are right now.

Tony Shepherd self-portrait with his daughter Katie (died 1994).
Photograph made as part of Reframing Grief workshop.

These eventually became a staple of the Active Grief Weekend retreats, residential weekends we designed to help other bereaved parents (and siblings) explore a creative response to grief. Key to the project is the idea that grief is about looking forward as much as it is about looking back. Yes, memories are all we have of a loved one who has died. But those memories and the story of their life still exist. They exist in the way we live our lives now. They exist in the relationship we still have with them, which though different, carries on. We don't stop loving them and the story of that love evolves in very much the same way that any love story evolves – with its ups and downs, heartaches and joys, jealousies and rage, anguish and laughter all mixed up in the neverending story that is grief. What we have found is that the new events in our lives following Joshua's death and the memories and stories they produced were as valuable and warranted as much photographic attention as the ones before his death. And that by continuing to represent our grief in this way we

are in a sense breathing new life into that fractured relationship. Joshua cannot respond, but he is still very much part of our imaginings, still very much part of our photographic work. We found this to be so empowering we wanted to share the idea with others.

Every photograph I make now helps to liberate the pain of our grief from the past.

The first outing for a Reframing Grief workshop was for our adopted charity, The Compassionate Friends, at one of their national gatherings in 2014. We ran two 90-minute sessions with twelve bereaved parents in each, most with very little practical experience of intentional photography, but all with a huge amount of stories and memories to share.

Our two disciplines seemed to gel well; Jane's as an experienced psychotherapist, mine as a photographer. Both therapy and photography are ways to seek beyond the surface and discover

Neil Hardy self-portrait with his son Tom (died 2014).
Photograph made as part of Reframing Grief workshop.

hidden emotions. While photography can have a more tangible result, they are both processes in which everyday realities can be tested and revealed anew. At least this was the approach we hoped to explore as the participants entered the room.

We had each of us brought favourite photos of our children and our first task was to tell the stories behind them and the memories they evoked. In the small groups we formed, words spilled out and across the room in a veritable hubbub, a cacophony even, of voices all (and I think this is the interesting bit) trying to describe their feelings. But at the same time the mere act of vocalising our thoughts, of telling the narrative, seemed to get in the way of really connecting with these

photos and the child within. In a sense, words were failing us.

At this point we asked people to remain in their groups but to sit quietly and merely observe their images, together and in silence. In the hush that followed Jane used her mindfulness techniques to encourage us to stay in the moment, however difficult the feelings, to try to lose a sense of time and to find a connection with our child that is now and something more than just memory. It was extraordinary, as the words disappeared and the emotions took over, hands felt for another to hold, an arm went around another's shoulder, tears began to form and, frankly, I was stunned.

> *Inspirational – I have been so sad that we have no new photographs of (our child) and now I feel I can put all our pictures into a new context.*
>
> *Feedback from a workshop participant*

Photographs, of course, are always memories – they are always of the past; of something that has already happened. You cannot take a photo of the future. But while they are always of the past, they are also always in the present. And like memory, their meaning or the meaning they have for us can evolve with time, sometimes radically and overnight. We recognised this in the photos we had brought of our children… innocent snapshots that have now become overloaded with longing and painful fantasies of what might have been.

There are two aspects to this business of exploring grief with photography. There are the photos we already have of our child who is now dead. Photos that were taken in all innocence of what the future might bring, now portals to our memories holding us close to a life that once was, both ours and theirs. And then there are the images that we can

make now – post tragedy – of the lives we now inhabit, both ours and theirs.

Take that picture we have of Josh with his eyes closed. It has now attained a kind of iconic status in the way in which we remember him. In the continually shifting process of trying to find meaning in our lives and in his death, it has also become a way of 'reinventing' him. I have found much comfort in being able to re-photograph Josh's image – it has taken me from the raw pain of the void created by his absence to a newer sense of a continued relationship with him. He is no longer here, but Josh remains a huge presence in my creative endeavour and very much part of my life.

For the second part of our workshop people divided into pairs and together attempted to create a photograph that reflected some of these concerns. In a way, what we were trying to do was to weld together the past and the present – the past with all its longings and the present full of our current

Left: Julie Palmer portrait with her son Ryan (died 2014). Above: Tracey Gray remembers her children Kayleigh / 33, Sarah / 22, Michael / 20. Photographs made as part of Reframing Grief workshop

Matthew Edwards constructing a photograph of his son Dylan (died 2015). Photograph made as part of Reframing Grief workshop

desires – and in so doing rebuild our sense of a future.

As all bereaved parents will know, when your child dies, you are immediately thrown into a world in which the future has very little meaning. But in this act of re-photographing our child's image we began to see some real therapeutic possibilities in the way we can continue our relationship with her/him with less pain. With the photographs we made, we could begin to imagine a time when we can look upon their face and smile again, and know there are more photos to come – many of which we haven't even dreamed about... yet.

In our workshops we concentrate on re-photographing an already existing image, but there are so many more ways of photographing our grief. For some, the image of their child still holds too many painful reminders, so they might want to focus on a more abstract sense of their grief. Grief is such a complex range of emotions that finding words to describe them often seems to

result in cliché, or seem very ordinary, nothing like what we are truly experiencing.

And this is where making new photographs can help to play a part. We can learn to express our thoughts and feelings in a language that is not so literal. By finding the visual metaphors that are unique to us and that express our grief, we can interpret our feelings and our experiences in our own way. This is a route to honesty, something others are bound to recognise. Despite the very solidity of a photograph (this did actually happen – this person did actually exist) the language of photography is very fluid, in that photos in themselves hold no particular meaning outside of the way they are viewed. But isn't that a bit like grief anyway – a constant slipping and sliding of feelings and emotions around a central fact, that our child has died?

'*Looking at my picture of (my child) was so hard... I have always thought I was so totally rubbish at photography and not really interested in it, but it has inspired me to do more in the future.*'

Feedback from a workshop participant

From the top: Mij Turnbull self-portrait with her son Michael (died 2017). Rhian Roberts photographed with her son Ceri (died 2016). Jessica Turrell remembering her son Matt (died 2018). Photographs made as part of Reframing Grief workshop

8
Loved and lost: Simon Bray

These two photographs both contain Simon Bray, first as a young boy pictured with his dad, then as a grown man. It's now part of his ongoing project, Loved and Lost.

hen my father died at Christmas, in 2009, it was a shock, although it shouldn't have been. Dad had been ill for many years, undergoing treatments and trials, his condition slowly deteriorating as the cancer took over. I should have seen it coming, but for whatever reason, I hadn't accepted that one day he wouldn't be here any longer. And then he was gone.

His absence was tangible. For a long time, I didn't know what to do with the space he had left behind. Nothing was ever going to fill it, but somehow I wanted to try to make sense of it. It's not something that is easy to translate into words. Even though I could express certain feelings within the context of counselling, as a young man without many peers with similar experience, I didn't know how to articulate and verbalise what I was experiencing to those around me.

Photography has this magical way of allowing us to project all those emotions and memories onto an image. Feelings that we struggle to put into words are held within an image, and as I looked through old photographs of my dad, it became clear that

Left: Simon Bray, first as a young boy pictured with his dad, then as a grown man

there was a power in returning to these images. I spoke with my mum and asked her to select a photograph of her and Dad that we could return to. She selected a photograph taken a few days after they were engaged, standing together at the top of St. Giles Hill, overlooking Winchester, where they had spent their married life. Mum and I went back to the spot where they had stood over 30 years before and we restaged the picture.

Afterwards, we recorded a conversation over a cup of tea. It was an emotional experience for Mum (and for me). Returning to the place of the original photograph was a sensory experience that had invited her to engage with memories and stories that I had not heard before. A new insight into the person of my dad through my mum's eyes, a beautiful story of a certain love that drew them together and held them as one until the day he died.

A few days later, I placed the two images side by side – the original and the restaged. The space that my dad had left felt huge. Using photography to show the passing of time in this way is not a new technique; it has been done many times before and will be used again in the future, but sitting there, seeing those two images with 30 years between them, was a demonstration of the absence that Dad's death had left us with.

From those simple beginnings grew the Loved and

Ceryl with her son Macsen, Lawrenny Quay, Pembrokeshire

Lost project, through which I have now told 25 stories with participants from all across the UK, each sharing their heartfelt tale of loss. The project has reached people all over the world through exhibitions, books, podcasts and press coverage, and with each new viewer the message is shared that loss is something we can talk about.

The project is a platform to share experiences that may well otherwise go unspoken, an invitation to return to a place, engage with the sights, sounds, smells and textures that may not have been experienced for half a lifetime. It's a chance to revisit the memories and actively remember the people who are no longer with us, and speak about them to me, a stranger, who knows what it's like to lose someone close to you, but wants to hear what it was like, in your unique experience.

I've spent nearly eight years working on Loved and Lost in its various forms, and for the first few I was convinced I was doing something nice for everyone else, that I was trying to translate the worst experience of my life into something positive.

Maybe I was doing that to some extent, but what I had created was an opportunity to speak with others who were grieving, to find a language with which to understand and express my own grief.

The process of taking part in the project offers participants permission to engage with grief, pain, memories and stories for which they may otherwise not have a defined outlet. In day-to-day life, the sense of loss and the range of emotions that come with that can take you by surprise, and we'll each have certain places, dates and occasions that offer a chance to focus on what has happened, but actually those are few and far between. Having the chance to intentionally be part of the project, to take the photos (which become mementos in themselves) and talk about those no longer with us was something that the participants really wanted to engage with.

Photography has an immediacy and sense of truth that other visual art forms don't have. The perception is that a photograph is a trusted document of a moment in time (even though technology enables us to do otherwise) and it

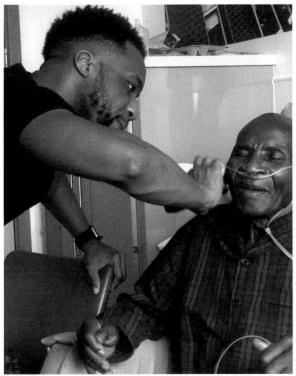

Kyle Campbell with his Granddad Bob

translates its narrative without any requirement for the viewer to have any prior knowledge of the medium. You don't need to have a discerning eye to understand most photographs, so it's very democratic in that sense, compared to painting, sculpture and film, which all have their own merits as means of expression and storytelling, but photography is the more ubiquitous medium.

Because of that, they're the things we have up in our houses, on mantelpieces, fridges and pinboards, and those family photographs become etched in our memories. I think for most of us, you can't be sure whether you remember a moment because of the moment itself or because someone took a photograph of it, and every time you see it, it alerts memories. Those aspects of truth and connection to memory allow us to engage with photographs emotionally and therefore they become invaluable (the thing we'd grab if the house caught fire).

Once someone has gone, the images of them become exponentially more important than before, and although they may be painful to look at, we keep them up in our houses, because the pain of remembering that they've gone is outweighed by the fear that we might forget them. The photographs invite us to remember – maybe they are the reason we remember – and the catharsis comes because we can't allow ourselves to forget.

The project became more poignant in 2018 when my younger sister passed away after a short illness. The context of the project meant that those around me knew it was something I wanted to talk about.

I don't think I'll ever understand loss, but that was never my aim. The beauty has been in the process and the searching, in the meeting of strangers, in the conversations over cups of tea, coffee and cake, and over pints in the pub, and in the power of photography to capture something that I had no other way of expressing.

We all have photographs that are loaded with memories and emotions. They make for great conversation starters.

9

What remains: Jimmy Edmonds

What do you see? What do I see? A young man's face and a pile of grit? There's the touch of a smile and a confident gaze that invites us to look beyond (behind) what could be volcanic debris. He's doing what I love to do… to close one eye and view the world differently. To see how it looks in two rather than three dimensions. To alter my perspective and line things up in my mind (my mind's eye) and produce another kind of order. I like hiding behind a tree or a door frame and in a sort of voyeuristic way see what only I can see – a kind of hide and seek with reality.

Is he hiding or seeking? He has laid his head to one side, resting, thoughtful, as if peeking out from behind the bedclothes after waking first thing in the morning, wondering what the day will bring.

The light on his face produces a subtle sheen. There's a glow, a radiance – a giveaway that perhaps this image is not quite what it seems at first sight – that it is an image within an image.

The photograph is of course a montage… a construct if you like. The eye and the smile and the colour belong to our son. The black and greyness in the foreground are his mortal remains, his ashes.

The image was one of my first intentional attempts to visualise my grief, to employ something of the craft I had come to respect as a particularly powerful means of expression. It was made some weeks after his death and was one of the very first to deal with the reality of his death, the absolute realness – the hard facts – that while I had life, he no longer did. Up until this point, we had fed off the hundreds (if not thousands) of photos and snapshots we had of him, desperate to keep his memory alive, to see him there smiling, laughing, pulling funny faces, all evidence that he was and still is our son, our brother, our friend.

Looking back at these memories, at this history, while it was an emotional necessity driven by an intense need to re-establish a sense of security, it was also a denial of the present. Was there a point when looking back became incompatible, discordant with our new reality – a reality in which for us Joshua was both alive and dead? We needed and still need his spirit, but to move forward in our grief we also needed to confront his absence, his not being here, his death.

Some weeks after his funeral, the undertakers had informed us that Josh's ashes were ready for collection. A few days later we found ourselves in possession of a very ordinary green plastic bottle containing our son's cremated remains. If you have also been in possession of a loved one's ashes, you will know that they are surprisingly heavy, a weighty substance that seems to negate the subtlety of spirit they represent. But if we

> **It's said that a photo will almost always outlive its subject matter.**

were to believe that these gritty bits of carbon had a history – that they did once belong to Josh and his body, to the physicality of his existence, then we must find a way to connect them to both his life and his death.

It's said that a photo will almost always outlive its subject matter. There's a sort of push me – pull you between the Joshua that still has life and the physical remains: the bits of carbon and bone that were once so much part of his aliveness, which can now only be but a testament to his one-time existence.

Turning to photography to accommodate this tension follows from the way photography works. Of all the visual arts, photography is perceived as a true record of reality – unlike a painting or a drawing, the subject must have existed for it to

59

have been photographed. John Berger calls this a 'thereness' of a photograph: you cannot take a photograph of something or someone that doesn't actually exist, that isn't there. Photographs have an authenticity, a veracity that seems to bring certainty to an uncertain world.

And yet they lie. Contrary to what we might think that a photograph tells us, its meaning is always in flux. Whatever the truth of a photograph at the time of making, the way we interpret it, the way we see it, is limited to frame and context and will change according to perception and over time. The boy I still see with the confident smile and a twinkle in his eye, the one who (this picture tells me) still breathes air and life, is dead. And as time passes, his photograph (maybe all photographs) becomes a greater and greater lie.

It is this confusion at the heart of photography, this chaos of meaning, that draws me to the medium. A photograph is both its subject and it isn't. This is Joshua (no mistaking that smile),

and it isn't. It shows me an image of Joshua who still has life, and yet he doesn't. It offers me what philosopher and literary theorist Roland Barthes called a 'perfect illusion', a deceiving image hiding behind (or in front of) an intractable reality. As an art form this photograph mirrors almost exactly my own bewilderment about Joshua being dead, of being 'not alive'.

We made many photographs that day. A good many of them became part of a larger project and a book, entitled *Released* that I published later that year.

As much as the final images now represent the story of our grief in those early days, the process of engaging with Joshua's image in a purposeful, intentional and creative way was a lesson in itself. I was learning that engaging directly with the reality/unreality of his death was going to be more therapeutic than shying away from painful feelings.

If I didn't know it before, I was discovering a new
potential for my photographic practice, one that
allowed me to find comfort in this not knowing,
or this refusal to know, this ambiguity of grief.
For grief is equivocal; always filled with doubt and
uncertainty. It's chaotic. And learning to accept
this chaos is fundamental to dealing with such
a traumatic loss.

Gillian Melling with her son Bruno, photo William Melling

‘*I couldn't paint until mid 2012, I was literally too emptied and detached.*’

10
Studio Wall: Gillian Melling

In June 2011, just after his 19th birthday, Gillian Melling's son Bruno left with three friends to go on holiday to Thailand. Already an accomplished photographer, he had just been offered a place on a photography degree at Glasgow School of Art. They had been gone four days when the police were at her door – Bruno, Conrad and Max had all been killed in a bus crash.

about three weeks after Bruno died, I woke up crying, and there in my bedroom was a cabbage white butterfly. The window and door were closed. How it got there I still cannot fathom. It was on the windowpane itself, directly above the pavement where I had last said goodbye to Bruno. I knew the butterfly was somehow Bruno and he was there with me, it was an incredible feeling. I took three photographs of the little butterfly on a phone.

When I finally managed to go into my studio it was the butterfly that helped me. I incorporated it into a painting I had previously been working on just before Bruno died, coincidentally, of a view from my bedroom window.

Over the next two years I painted and drew over 300 portraits of Bruno, some small-scale and some

Bruno Melling

Bruno, oil on canvas

large, some from imagination, some from photographs. At times it was gruelling when I couldn't 'find' his likeness or expression. I wanted him to be close to us all the time and not to be forgotten.

I make my own oil paint and canvases as I like the process and pace, it keeps me embedded with the natural pigments, oils and materials. The soft viscosity of oil paint, colour, layering, composition and mark can, I believe, potentially hold emotion, love, worry, sorrow, joy, beauty and life itself. It is sometimes magical how an image can evolve from paint and a brush or rag. I approach my work intuitively and do not plan ahead in any detail as I need the process of image-making to be a journey where many changes can happen. Oil paint is the perfect medium for this.

My paintings are essentially figurative, with elements of abstraction. Narrative, memories and

feelings are always there, but sometimes hidden. After Bruno died, we found a few photographs of him that we had never seen before, including one of him posing in a boxer stance. In the painting, Studio Wall, I surrounded this image with others on my studio wall. I wanted this work to be a safe and magical world for him, as my studio is for me. It has references to Diego Velázquez's Las Meninas, a painting with a complex and enigmatic composition that raises questions about reality and illusion. I love that it has an uncertain relationship between the viewer and figures in the painting.

A reference to Las Meninas is to the right of my painting. Judy Garland is there, part of a montage birthday card Bruno's sister made for his 19th birthday. There is a Glasgow tourist map and a reference to Renfrew Street and the School of Art where he was due to start on the return from holiday. I've added speckles of silver, the pavement

when words are not enough

Left: Barba x 8 (and butterfly)
Right: Studio Wall – both
oil on canvas

about asking permission to photograph them, but eight shops agreed to take part and he created an amazing collection of images full of atmosphere, colour and texture, all testimony to the kind of curiosity that makes a good photographer.

Over the years I have incorporated images and colours from Bruno's many photographs into my work. I feel very privileged as this keeps me connected to him, essentially seeing through his eyes, in the present.

I feel drawn towards paintings I can 'travel' into and around and find things along the way. I wanted to combine the eight barbers from Bruno's book into a sparkling scape of colour and paint and to have no image pinned down or over-defined, and no one as the point of focus.

Now and again, I revisit the places in his photographs to record the changes over the years. The butterfly still appears from time to time.

The personal nature of my work means it doesn't sell well, but that is how it is. The quiet world of painting may have left me financially insecure, but it has always, always given me sanctuary. Now in grief it takes me to a peaceful place of contemplation, meaning, tussle and learning. I am starting to incorporate more abstraction in my painting to imagine a parallel world and space alongside this world. I will always incorporate Bruno's work, my family and memories into these landscapes. I am looking forward to this.

where we last said goodbye, the three stars of Orion's belt, and three candles for the three friends. Mementos of trauma that we have endured.

Bruno was an aspiring and committed photographer. He left behind a work with a deep social conscience, honesty and warmth. Living in Waterloo and close by the River Thames, he made a series of studies of the river, contrasting its immense natural form and its silent presence with the urban landscape of central London. He also documented the creeping gentrification and social cleansing of the wider neighbourhood of South London, photographing and commenting on how many of his friends felt as they were forcibly moved out from their council homes.

For his Foundation course, the project that got him into the degree course at Glasgow School of Art, Bruno created 'Barba', a book of photographs made in various barber shops in London. He had become fascinated by the quiet and intimate world of Italian barber shops in the capital. He was nervous

11
A brush with grief: Lize Kruger

*Lize with her
son Francois*

***Lize Kruger lost her only son, Francois,
to suicide in 2008. Already an established
artist, she moved to the UK from South
Africa. She now uses her art primarily
as therapy, questioning herself, her role
as a mother and all the feelings of
fragmentation and destruction that
come after a decade of battling with
loss and grief.***

Some people say they don't want
to be defined by their child's
death, but I didn't want my child
to be defined by his death. He is
so much more than that. But I started to define
myself by his death. In some ways, I'm more and
in some ways I am less a person than I was then.

When I was asked to describe my grief journey,
I looked back into my diary notes of the past
twelve years. I found loads of questions, not asking
why my precious son died, but why was I still alive.

These are some of the notes I found.

I'm scared.
I'm terrified of the year ahead.
I'm afraid of myself.
I'm scared of the United Kingdom.
I'm scared of South Africa.
I don't belong anywhere anymore.
I'm scared of and for my children.
I'm scared of life.
I'm not scared of death.
My brain is devouring me.
How can I escape from myself?!
I lost a huge part of my vocabulary.
I lost all my confidence.
I lost all interest in beauty.
I became obsessed with my children.
I became a useless partner.
I lost my creativity and the urge to create.
I became scared of life and scared of myself.
I stumbled around in the wilderness and meekly
tried to navigate in the darkness.
What's wrong with me?
Why can't I find inner joy?
Why do I feel a complete and utter failure?
Why don't I have any self-confidence anymore?
Why do I feel so useless?
Why do I live?
Why don't I have any trust in my
abilities anymore?
I lost a huge part of my memory.
Where is Lize?

Above: Nothing made sense anymore II, digital collage

Left: A delicate betrayal III, mixed media/ digital collage
Opposite: Testing my Resilience II,
archival print, all Lize Kruger

I became utterly fearful and riddled with anxiety. After the first two years, when the shock started to lift, my mind slowly but steadily deteriorated into a place where it haunted me. With self-hate and sabotage. Depression and extreme anxiety almost cost me my own life.

Still, I had to keep up appearances, because my family has been through so much heartache, so much pain, so much trauma that I could not do that to them as well. Depression has its own voice, and it tells you that it will be better for everyone if you leave, that you are becoming more and more of a liability to everyone around you.

It became impossible for me even to try to be creative, and for all intents and purposes, I put my brushes down and thought I'd never work again. But with the worldwide lockdown during the pandemic, something changed for me. I suddenly felt the world had regressed to my level, and I didn't feel like the alien anymore. For more than twelve years I had worn a daily mask, pretending to be coping and surviving while I felt dead inside. Using a physical mask, with others around me having to do it too, strangely felt very comforting to me.

I started to search for the meaningful: the little gems that can carry me through the abyss. I began to experiment with new art forms, and one experiment leads to another.

During my grief process, I went into total shutdown. There were a lot of times that I experienced it as if I was splitting in two, and it took immense work, willpower and resilience to try to combine those two or even more elements of my persona again.

It took more than ten years to integrate my separated psyche with myself again.
At first I became utterly fearless, and then

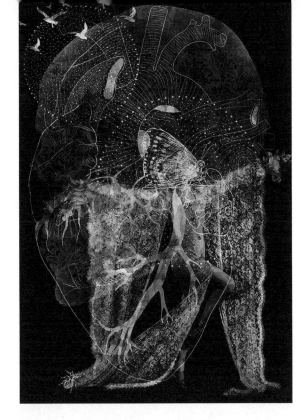

And now I realise how far I have come and what a huge role the current pandemic played in my rediscovery of myself.

I find it important to highlight mental health issues and any injustices regarding children through my work. I want to believe that my work will succeed in this and hopefully add value to our society or the life of someone else.

A delicate betrayal

I always worked in physical layers. However, it is an extremely expensive way to create if it is not a commission. That is why I started to experiment with digital tools. This way I could incorporate different layers and still convey the messages I wanted to.

Why layers? For me, nothing is ever what it seems to be. There will always be more to life, a person or situation than meets the eye. We are products of layers of experiences, thoughts and influences and I love the effect that different layers create on those below. Shadows that create new images and with different light, almost developing lives of their own. I approach all my work from this viewpoint.

Nothing made sense anymore

The figure in Nothing Made Sense Anymore is actually a drawing I did from an old vintage anatomical drawing. When I finished, I was shocked to see how much I had made it look like Francois. The last image of Francois that is burned into my brain was exactly that – his face to the side on my lap while we were racing to the hospital.

The work emphasises the discord between heart and brain when a person is psychologically broken by depression. I know his mind was completely fragmented by that time and I could see the pain and conflict he was going through.

Testing My Resilience

Testing My Resilience was created to illustrate the daily effort I had to administer during Covid. Not being able to see my daughters and granddaughters in South Africa and New Zealand was very hard. However, against the light of so much pain in the past and being surrounded by a world that is experiencing loss on a daily basis, I force myself to 'dance' until the day I see them again.

12
L'Accordéon de la Mémoire: Cassie Toulouse

Cassie Toulouse's daughter Ella died in April 2020, aged 23, after being diagnosed with a rare cancer in the same year. Cassie lives in Paris and took part in one of our Active Grief Weekends in 2021.

Cassie, right, with her daughter Ella

As humans, I believe we have a vital need to create narratives about who we are, where we come from and where we are going. They ground us and connect us to others and to the incomprehensible fabric of our existence, giving meaning and coherence to the inexplicable.

After our daughter Ella died at 23 from a rare and aggressive cancer in the space of four months, we combed through everything she left us, every belonging, written word and creation, every detail of her medical history, starting even before she was born, in our search for signs and clues both physical and spiritual for some coherence to the trajectory of her life. The mission was to create a narrative around her life, as if by framing it we could keep our own lives from spinning out of control and hold our family together despite our boundless pain.

Accordéon de la Mémoire is a small work painted by Ella when she was 16. It is a ten-page, unbound book that unfolds like an accordion, in which Ella captures episodes, inspirations and little treasures from her childhood. In this leporello, or folded book, her mind and paintings jump around in time, yet are bookended by scenes of her birth and a self-portrait of her younger self painting the work. It is graphic, humorous and colourful and a sensitive testimony to childhood and the pleasures and hardships of growing up. It tells a story.

Above: the bound book. Below: Cassie with
L'Accordéon de la Mémoire

During the shock of the first year after her death, while I struggled every morning to get up and couldn't accept that my daughter had become a memory, my husband Jean-Baptiste suggested we work, as a family, on a project, something to 'turn our inside pain out,' something to honour Ella. Because of Covid we had been deprived of any opportunity to share our grief with friends and relatives, and in particular with Ella's own friends. We imagined sending a gift from her, something to treasure, to keep her close. A replica of an artwork? Everything about Ella was artistic, and she spoke most fluently in images, but she was very unassuming and never claimed to be an artist. We knew some of her works but had no idea of how prolific she really was. After she died, we found hundreds and hundreds of ink and gouache works that she had kept to herself, all carefully preserved in notebooks and folders, stashed away in her closet. Of all these works, though, it was

L'Accordéon that spoke the loudest, as if Ella understood the power of stories and somehow knew she wouldn't always be here to reminisce. It became obvious that a replica of this work would be our gift.

Jean-Baptiste found a fantastic publisher and art book printer and worked hours and hours with them to get everything right: colours, format, comments, fonts, packaging, and so on. With our other children we interpreted as best we could the depictions and allusions on each page and recorded them in a booklet to be cleverly attached to each replica. Each replica was tied together with a purple ribbon and placed in a customised cardboard box for shipping. A little more than a year after Ella died, we sent a package out to everyone she and we cared about with a letter explaining what it was and how it came about. It was a family labour of love.

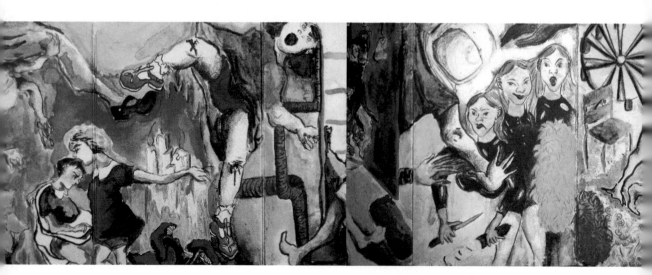

L'Accordéon and our publishing project help tether us to the world Ella left and that we must now navigate without her. It's almost like Ella created it in preparation for what was to come, a little story within her larger story, to set us on the soothing path of creating a narrative around her life. In the letter we sent out with L'Accordéon, we wrote, 'We feel she would have wanted us to share it with friends and the people she cared about – it is a gift from her to you. We hope you enjoy it as much as we do, and leave it open on a shelf rather than tucked away in its cardboard case, letting Ella's benevolent presence bring forth a smile when you get a glimpse of it.'

Giving Ella's work a new life and letting it tell a part of her story, bringing a smile from time to time in different homes across the world, helps, a little bit.

Below from left to right: Details from pages of L'Accordéon de la Mémoire: It all begins with a birth; Ella Toulouse = E.T. Phone home. As a little girl, Ella was fascinated by Mars and dreamed of being an astronaut; She would hang tea bags from her bedroom window; Snuggled in her duvet is Lucien, the little white mouse she secretly raised in her bedroom; Back to Mom, who has prepared a bowl of noodles and the pilfering blue hand; Ella as a little girl absorbed in her drawing – a frame-within-the-frame.

13
Out of time:
Jimmy Edmonds

After the initial freeze of those first few weeks and months, when making any kind of creative work was just too much to contemplate, the urge to find a way to express our feelings of grief began to gain strength. For me, dreaming up photographic projects became a preoccupation. Those who mourn a loved one will inevitably turn to the family album and all those snapshots that tell the story of that person's life. Of all the many hundreds of images we had of Josh, I kept returning to what we now called his 'sleepy picture'. In many cultures there's a soothing association with sleep that attempts to blur the distinction between life and death. If for the moment I find it easier to deny his death, perhaps reworking this image can ease my way to an acceptance of this cruel dichotomy – the yawning gulf between the Joshua then and the Joshua now. His physical being, the vessel that was his body, is gone but his essence lingers on.

To rework this image of Joshua I started looking at some alternative photographic techniques and discovered that the process of making anthotypes would fit some of my concerns.

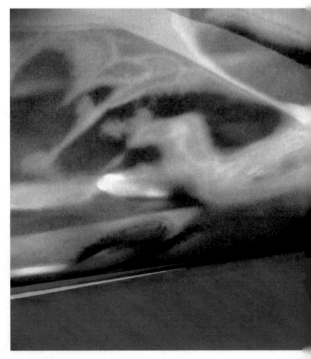

An anthotype is an image created by a long-neglected process using a photosensitive solution made from plants. An emulsion is made from crushed flower petals (or any other light-sensitive plant, fruit or vegetable) that is then used to coat

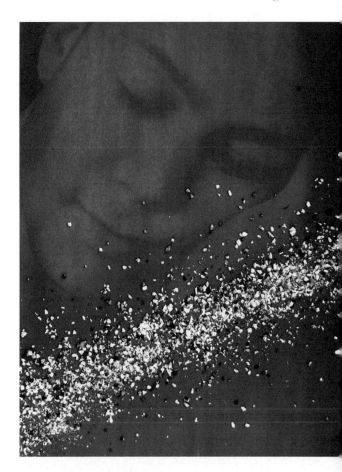

a sheet of paper. The image is produced by laying transparent material over the paper so that when exposed to direct and full sunlight the emulsion will fade in those areas where the light gets through. But there is a drawback: unlike other photographic prints, anthotypes cannot be fixed. Unless stored in a cool dark place, the fading process will continue, and eventually the image will completely disappear.

I learned this from a fellow photographer when, in November 2011, just nine months after Josh had died, I was invited to take part in a local photography exhibition, Beyond the Comfort Zone. I was interested in using natural ingredients to make these images, in using a process that had history to it but had long since died out. As a technique it seemed to have more in common with making elderflower wine than manipulating grains of halides or pixels on a computer screen. That the images wouldn't last, that the natural process of decay would mean I would have to confront again the consequence of letting them go.

To make these images, I used the juice squeezed from raw beetroots grown in our garden. Then positive transparencies were made from various digital files we had of Josh, including his 'sleepy picture', and some photos I had of my own father who had died 20 years or so previously and never knew his grandson. Once the paper had dried, I laid the transparencies on top and mounted them together before placing them in the sun to expose.

My father (died 1987) and my son (died 2011)

Even before Josh died, I had become interested in the way photography became a medium for memorialising the dead. In the latter half of the nineteenth century the middle classes could, for the first time, afford an authentic visual record of their nearest and dearest. The family album of the twentieth century – snapshots of weddings, bar mitzvahs, holidays in the sun – was still a long way off, so post-mortem photography became a thing. In our modern era, there's a taboo about recording a dead person's face. To have photographed Josh in his casket would have been too much for me and I'm not sure I would've wanted anyone else to take that picture, though the image is imprinted in my mind.

The anthotype project developed as a substitute for this omission. It was also a way of exploring the way photographs exist within a time frame, especially now that time, for me, had become a somewhat vague concept. All photographs are a moment in time, and we too had to a certain extent been stopped in time. Yet the world continued to move forward and I wanted to explore our sense of being in time, while Josh is now out of time.

What could my experiments with anthotypes say about this discontinuity, this absence of time?

If a regular photo is made in the fraction of a second, an anthotype will need an exposure time of days, even weeks. If a photographic print or

how to make an anthotype

Anthotypes are easy to make. The process is followed in three steps: making the emulsion, preparing the canvas and printing.

You will need
- Petals from a colourful flower, raw vegetables, berries or other plants
- Mortar and pestle or electric food blender
- Cheesecloth, coffee filter, cotton cloth or very fine masked strainer
- Glass container or ceramic bowl for mixing ingredients
- Water (distilled if possible) or alcohol
- Watercolour paper
- Paintbrush
- Acetate or transparency film in sheets
- A large size positive (not negative) or items to make photograms
- Glass clip-frame or contact print frame
- Sunshine

1 Make the emulsion
An anthotype emulsion can be made from any number of plant materials. Grind, mash or blend the petals, roots or pulp with a pestle and mortar or electric blender then strain the resulting 'soup' through a cheesecloth or coffee filter into a bowl. If the resulting 'mash' is too dry, dilute it a little with water or alcohol.

2 Prepare the canvas
You can use any paper that will hold the emulsion, though since it will be out in the sun for a good while, the sturdier the better, such as watercolour paper. There are two ways of applying the emulsion onto the paper; painting with a brush can leave brush strokes on the paper, adding a handmade quality, while dipping the paper into the solution will give you a more even coat. It's advisable to work in a dimly lit area as any sunlight will begin to degrade the colour of your emulsion. Similarly, leave the paper to dry in the dark.

3 Printing the anthotype
For a photographic image you will need to create a positive monochrome (black and white) transparency of the image you want to use. Clear acetate transparency film normally used for overhead projectors is available in A4 and A3 sheets either for inkjet or laser printers. You will need to create a digital file to print from or scan the photo directly on the printer. Remember, the transparency needs to be the same size as the final anthotype. Carefully lay the acetate on the dried art paper, emulsion side up, then insert both in a clean glass picture frame. Leave in the sun for about a week. You might like to check on progress – it's hard to resist and it's wonderful to see the resulting image gradually appearing – but be extra careful when peeling the transparency back and make sure you lay it down again in exactly the same register.

*Right: anthotype in 2011 and below, what
they look like now, years later*

digital file has the potential to last forever and
will more often than not outlive its subject, an
anthotype will fade in a matter of months. I was
drawn to this idea of photographic impermanence.
Rather than an unassailable record of a person's
life, the photograph as anthotype becomes, just
like us, a transitory object.

I was also conscious of the speed with which in
the last two decades the world of photography has
transitioned from film to digital with massive

implications for the way we make, take,
manipulate and view photographs. I felt a huge
need to slow down and give myself the time to
reflect on the significance that Josh's image, his
photographic likeness, now has for me.

As a measure of his temporal existence, I embedded
some of Joshua's ashes into the anthotypes, so that
by the time his image had faded away all that
remained was, in fact, all that remains.

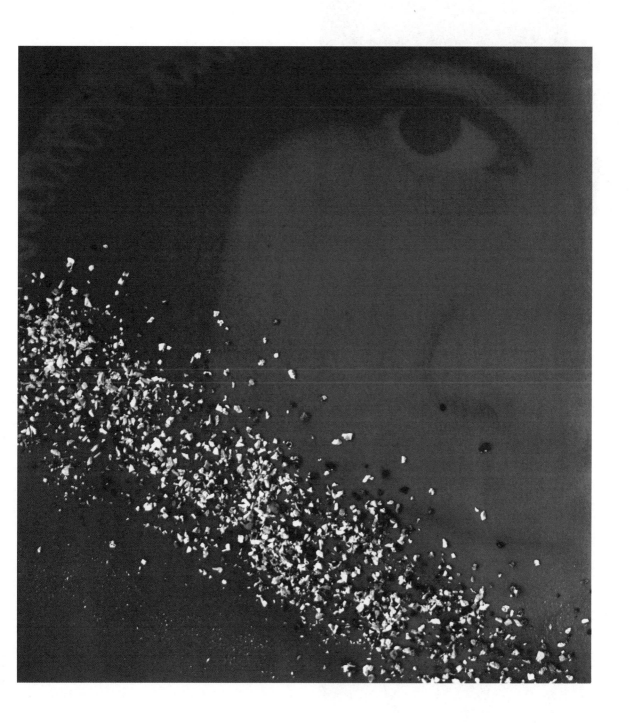

Gary Andrews with his partner Joy
and children Lily and Ben

14
A doodle a day:
Gary Andrews

19.2.19

Going through an old rucksack today, I unexpectedly came across one of your scarves. It still smelled of you. This didn't produce tears or sadness however, but rather smiles, love and gratitude that you were part of my life.

x♡x

When Gary Andrews' wife Joy died suddenly in 2017, his practice of drawing a doodle a day became his way of managing his grief. Known on social media as @garyscribbler, he is a professional illustrator and animator with a career stretching back through numerous filmmaking credits (including Fireman Sam, The World of Peter Rabbit, and We're Going on a Bear Hunt) to the time he left art school in 1983.

Back then, the media were all very traditional – pen and ink, watercolour, marker pens. As time has gone by, the work has changed and in recent years I mainly found myself drawing on the computer. To re-connect with the basics, I decided in April 2016 to keep a daily doodle diary in a sketchbook, using a pen. No rough drawing first, just straight in with the pen, recording my observations and thoughts and never taking longer than 15 minutes for a drawing. It was really an exercise in technique, using the

3.3.19.

When a little girl has concerns and needs some guidance from Daddy...
...Daddy always thinks "What would you say?"

2.11.18.

So last night I made a decision. I moved my wedding ring to the other hand. A symbol of our love. Always remembered, but time to move forwards. You are gone and I can't change that. I will always love you, but need to acknowledge that life has changed.

And I know you understand. You always knew best!

20.6.19

Ugh. No difference. Why isn't this diet working?

You do realise a 'diet' consists of more than just eating salad for one day, right?

Drawings and photos by Gary Andrews

> *The act of sitting and 'unpacking' my feelings each day really helped me to let go of some of the pain: getting it down on paper, exorcising those demons that can gnaw away in the darkness.*

diary aspect to make sure I didn't skip a day. Then, in October 2017, my life was turned upside down when my beautiful wife Joy died suddenly from sepsis, leaving me a widower with two kids aged seven and ten.

At this point, the daily drawings became a part of my routine. Always last thing at night, they were a moment of mindfulness to reflect on my day. It seemed natural to me to continue drawing every day, but now it became a way for me to process my grief. The act of sitting and 'unpacking' my feelings each day really helped me to let go of some of the pain: getting it down on paper, exorcising those demons that can gnaw away in the darkness.

I also documented the journey with my children – both the grief moments and the funny, solo-parent ones as well. The kids had always enjoyed my daily doodles and now would often look back through the sketchbooks – reliving fun memories and seeing their own grief journey. They would comment on how their feelings had changed over the weeks and months.

Often in the drawings, Joy would (and still does) turn up, commenting on things that were happening in our life – symbolising the ongoing conversations I still have with her in my head – the bonds so strong that death was unable to break them. The kids always like it when that

happens, she is still so present in our lives. After a while, the social media postings got noticed, leading to radio, TV and podcast appearances and a large online following. Eventually this also led to me publishing a book, a collection of the doodles called *Finding Joy*.

I have a loyal and engaged following, with whom I have the most beautiful interactions as they share their own stories with me or thank me for putting down on paper things that they were finding hard to explain or cope with. Knowing my drawings are helping others has also helped me. It has made Joy's death less pointless and has been a huge part of my own healing process.

Recently I have been asked to lead several online workshops talking about using creativity (specifically daily 'doodling') as a form of self-counselling. Creativity – and art in particular – has been a huge part of my grief journey, helping me form a positive relationship with those feelings. It is something I feel strongly about and continue to promote as a way to help others who may be struggling to come to terms with what has happened to them. Being able to do this, I feel very blessed.

Finding Joy, Gary Andrews (Hodder & Stoughton, 2021)

Deirdre Nolan with photo of her daughter Laoise

15
Celebrating Laoise: Deirdre Nolan

Deirdre and Liam Nolan's daughter Laoise had lived with a rare form of leukaemia her whole life. She died in 2016, aged nine.

When Laoise died, it was a shock. I really was not prepared for it. It hit us like a bus, full on. We had known for the previous five years that her leukaemia wasn't treatable and when the end finally came, it was sudden, unexpected, visceral. I thought I might have been prepared but I was completely wrong.

We had to gather ourselves and be present for Michael, her eleven-year-old brother. That was hard, but so necessary. We had to be there for each other. But how could we be there for Laoise when she was no longer with us? We were still her parents. How could we connect with her now that she was absent? I don't remember even asking that question at the time… it was just a gut feeling that there had to be more than this emptiness. We knew she was gone but we couldn't make sense of it. We wanted to cling on to her in whatever way we could.

It started when Liam made an album with photos, words and music from Laoise's Celebration Day; a day when we were joined by family, friends,

neighbours and the whole of Laoise's village school. The day helped us to say goodbye to Laoise while we felt wrapped up and enveloped in the love of our families and the community. The album reminds us of how much Laoise was loved, not just by us but by her extended family and many friends and neighbours. We asked them to write little letters to Laoise so we could read their thoughts later, and we added them to the album too.

When that was completed, Liam, in particular, was determined to keep going, grasping that connection with Laoise with all his might.

Cushion covers made from Laoise clothes

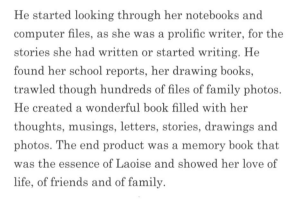

Left: dried flower bookmarks. Right: pompoms to celebrate Laoise's life

He started looking through her notebooks and computer files, as she was a prolific writer, for the stories she had written or started writing. He found her school reports, her drawing books, trawled though hundreds of files of family photos. He created a wonderful book filled with her thoughts, musings, letters, stories, drawings and photos. The end product was a memory book that was the essence of Laoise and showed her love of life, of friends and of family.

As for me, I love crafting and making, so my connection with Laoise continued when I decided that I would like to make cushions for each family member using fabric from some of Laoise's t-shirts. We had been saving her clothes to make a quilt for her bed but at that point, I couldn't bring myself to cut up her lovely dresses. Maybe one day I will be brave enough. She had so many t-shirts and a lot of them had been given to her as gifts. I was able to make cushion covers from the pictures or prints on the front of the t-shirts and give the cushions to the people who had gifted her the t-shirts. I also made memory cushions where I cut the t-shirt fabrics into the shape of leaves and used the fabric from her Obi-Wan Kenobi cape to cut out tree trunks. The result was a cushion cover with a tree pattern on it made out of fabric that people would remember her wearing. While it was important for me to be making something out of items that Laoise wore – oh how familiar all those patterns were – I think I also wanted others to have something to remember Laoise by. I didn't want anyone to forget her.

Last year, I collected, pressed and dried wildflowers growing around her grave in the green cemetery and from some of the flowers she had planted in our garden. On her anniversary this year, I used the pressed flowers to make bookmarks for the family.

Every year, I ask her friends and our family members to make a pompom so that I can create a decoration to hang on the wall of the house. Anyone passing by, who was at her Celebration Day, will know that the decoration is there to remind us of Laoise and to celebrate the wonderful little girl that she was – bright, bold, colourful and most definitely unique.

16
Grief, craft and nature: Jim Clabon

Jim Clabon's daughter Phoebe died of hydrocephalus in 2019. Since then, he has learned a new craft that has taken him closer to nature and closer to his ancestors.

We held our eleven-year-old daughter Phoebe's funeral service in a privately owned woodland not far from our home. An ancient woodland with a mixture of established broad-leaved trees, coppiced hazel and some new oaks that were planted after the storm in the late 1980s. In its centre stands a very large, old beech tree; it was around this tree that we held Phoebe's funeral service.

In the early days of my grief, this was a place I could go to be alone with my thoughts. I'd leave home with the intention of going to work but I often just kept driving and ended up in those woods, not feeling able to face the people and places of my old life. I spent a fair bit of time sat by the fire reading about grief and learning about the trees in the woodland, how to look after them and what our ancestors used them for. The language I found around grief often didn't do justice to how I was feeling, but those woods somehow offered me a language I could understand.

I started learning green woodworking a few months after Phoebe died; I recognised that I needed to keep my hands and mind busy. My mantra was 'do something'.

Nature is full of life and death. Grieving through Covid, in a time where we could touch nothing, I found myself in this place of living things that needed to be touched. It felt like a comfortable place to be. The woodland offered me a reprieve from the chore of grief, but it also allowed me to face my grief in a gentler environment.

The relationship between my craft and grief is more complicated than just those two parts, it's tied up with the experience of being in nature and learning its ways. Specifically, the ways of that place, a place that witnessed and seems to hold a memory of the day we brought our daughter to it to mark her ending.

First, I made a shave horse, a device that you sit on to clamp a piece of wood with your feet. Then, with your hands free, you use a drawknife to shape a piece of wood to make a spoon or stool. It's a lovely thing to sit in the woods and shape a piece of wood. Then came the pole lathe made from a large ash tree, it's powered by my leg and a long springy pole that brings the pedal back up. I also built a small workshop with some of the oak that was in need of thinning out.

Opposite: Jim Clabon and his daughter Phoebe. Left: Jim in his woodland studio. Below: A bowl with a special connection to Phoebe

There is a tradition in these woods to thank them for the wood that we use. In doing so, I think of the life that tree has had and what it has offered us, what it has given up and what it will become. It gives me a level of appreciation for nature and what we take from it, but it also enables me to find the similarities between their existence and ours and the parallels to my daughter's life.

Around this time, I was having trouble sleeping. We'd chosen to donate Phoebe's organs and it was this procedure that had got lodged in my mind. I'd lie in bed at night playing it in detail over and over, going through all the events leading up to her death.

The pole lathe was made from an ash tree that had stood for about 70 years on the edge of the wood. An ash tree can live for 400 years, so this one, like Phoebe, died young. I thought of what it had witnessed in its time. Being on the edge of the woodland it was on the frontline of any incoming storms. I recognised the protection it offered the other trees. I thanked it and proceeded to make the component parts I needed for the pole lathe. At some point through that process, I wondered if the surgeons that operated on Phoebe showed the same respect that I had shown to this ash tree. Maybe it was my responsibility to have had those conversations, to have been with her while she went through that procedure, to thank her for what she had given to us and the gift she was

giving to her unknown recipients. Was this the reason I was having those flashbacks? I'm not sure, but after that day they stopped.

Now I make bowls on the pole lathe; they are beautiful objects and something our ancestors would be very familiar with. Every home would have had a wooden bowl made in this way. Nowadays it's a rare thing to have something that you know the origins of so well.

There is a purity to these objects. I enjoy the process, first walking around the wood looking for a suitable fallen branch, then working with an axe to carve out the basic shape. You are forced to work with the grain and 'imperfections' until you end up with a finished piece. For me, each tool mark represents a step forward in my grief journey.

I don't sell my work, some I've kept for use at home, but mostly I give them away to the people that have in some way walked with us.

17
A scintillating space:
Sangeeta Mahajan

Sangeeta Mahajan is a consultant anaesthetist at Guy's & St Thomas' Hospital in London. Her son Sagaar died in 2014, aged 20. She now describes herself as a mental health activist and educator. In 2021 Sangeeta contributed to our documentary film Beyond the Mask with the memorable comment: 'Our death happens to other people… My son's death is happening to me because I'm the one who has to live it.'

On the first Saturday in September 2014, I attended a flower-arrangement exhibition in Croydon at the invitation of my friend, Heena, who spent all her free time on a Japanese art form, Ikebana, and talked about it incessantly. The arrangements seemed to be floating in the air. Not a thing was out of place. Everything complemented everything else and they were displayed in shapely earthenware vases. I was struck by their simple elegance.

At that time my son Saagar was being treated for depression at home in London. We had decided that he would take a year out of university to allow for his rest and recovery. I was working full-time and looking after him. On the 16 October that year, he wrote me a note saying he 'couldn't take

it anymore' and ended his own life. He was 20.

The next six months were spent in India with family. I mostly sat still, watching the waves of an ocean, or the shapes in the sky, or the mist in the mountains or nothing at all.

On my return to London I slowly started work and every evening I fell asleep on the train coming home and missed my station. Work left me exhausted. The same job that I had enjoyed all my adult life was now a real slog. There was nothing I looked forward to. My heart and mind were in the past, bargaining with Time and Destiny.

That's when Heena suggested I try out Ikebana. I remembered the impact the minimalistic beauty of Ikebana had had on me. I signed up. The teacher, Mrs Patel, was a gentle lady of great repute. There were seven other students who had been learning for a while – women of all ages. They were calm and pleasant. Mrs Patel drew schematic diagrams on a whiteboard, explaining the name, function, quality and significance of each component of an arrangement. She emphasised the relationship between different parts, but mostly she spoke of the importance of spaces between them.

Wood symbolised mountains, while grasses and flowers suggested water. A natural landscape in a single vase. It was a meditation of sorts,

Opposite: Sangeeta Mahajan with her son Sagaar. Right: Ikebana – spaces, light, movement. Photos, Sangeeta Mahajan

exploring the relationship between the sky, humans and earth, between the outdoors and indoors, between the past, present and future. It was about harmony and the laws of nature, a welcome break from the cacophony of London. I looked forward to the day of the lessons.

'Not only beautiful flowers but also buds and withered flowers have life, and each has its own beauty. Be aware of the spaces you create. Spaces make your arrangement dynamic, allowing each flower and leaf to shine. They bring a lightness and movement to the table.' I saw her demonstrate this and every time it was magic.

Beauty heals. Through the last seven years, this practice has given expression to my feelings, it

has given me access to the joy and peace within me. I have rediscovered my creative potential and my ability to learn a new skill. It has helped me re-establish my faith in life and become part of a new loving community. It has brought home the fundamental truth of impermanence.

Ma is a Japanese word that can be roughly translated as 'gap', 'space' or 'pause'. It is best described as a simultaneous awareness of form and non-form, bringing the 'seen' into a sharper focus because of the presence of the 'unseen'. Saagar's physical absence has slowly transformed itself into an ethereal, scintillating space that gives prominence to the love and blessings that are present in my life. Whatever manifests in this space I witness with grace and gratitude.

89

18
On social media: Jane Harris and Jimmy Edmonds

Grief is an act of rebellion. In a grief-phobic and death-denying society, psychotherapist Francis Weller sees grief as a subversive act, a form of deep resistance to the disconnected way in which we have been conditioned to relate to the world. Grief, he suggests, 'undermines our society's quiet agreement that we will behave and be in control of our emotions. It is an act of protest that declares our refusal to live numb and small.' (*The Wild Edge of Sorrow*, Francis Weller)

Grief is chaotic but it also offers what Oscar Wilde called a 'wild alchemy' that relocates pain and suffering onto fertile ground. Historically and traditionally grief has always been communal, a shared experience that binds communities together in times of adversity, but in modern times grief has become more private, hidden from the public gaze and consequently from others who could help us heal, as well as for the creative opportunities that the open expression of grief could present. For much of contemporary society grief goes against the grain.

At the same time, in the last two to three decades there has been a huge shift in the way the world has interconnected. What was analogue is now digital. In photographic parlance, the light-sensitive grains of silver halides have been superseded by pixels producing digital images using the binary coding that has become the basis of all computer processing, and by extension the dominant way we all communicate with one another. What was once printed by hand is now infinitely reproduceable and consumed almost instantly.

And this helps us as we find new ways to share our grief. The world wide web and the internet have created radically different (some would say more democratic) ways of forming communities that don't necessarily rely on neighbourhood – communities that are based on interest rather than geography. More than anything it has enabled us to feed into and be fed by a bereavement community.

'People don't die online...' this was Josh's friend Jessica (see contribution on page 94) as she responded not just to the news of his death but to the way the internet has seeded new attitudes, new conversations and new ways of remembering the deceased.

The day after Josh died one of his colleagues was on the train to work and scrolling down his Facebook feed to find it full of shocked comments from literally hundreds of friends across the world. 'This was grief aired publicly, immediately and emotively,' Tom Kihl wrote in his own blog, 'before the news of his death even had the chance to sink in.' Already a conversation had started up, heartfelt words communicated via a platform so

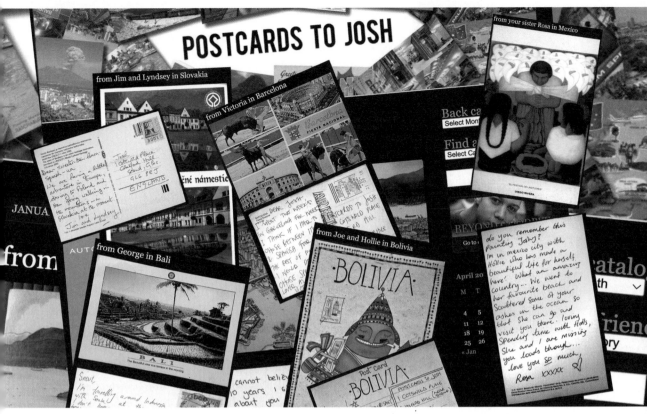

POSTCARDS TO JOSH

Postcards to Josh – taking Josh around the world

new (this was eleven years ago!) our society hadn't worked out what was and wasn't acceptable to post in this kind of situation.

If death is not a subject that society is traditionally very happy talking about, the range of communication tools we now have – literally at our fingertips – means the topic now unavoidably finds itself being discussed in the most public of arenas. We could worry that in those first few minutes of grief people may leave what can appear to others to be inappropriate posts. Using lots of exclamation marks or coming over as overly chatty, almost continuing the lighthearted text-speak banter they used to fire off. The exchange doesn't capture the gravity of the situation, and some may feel it's the ultimate indignity of our cult of the individual. Tom was himself worried that writing a blog post about the development of social media etiquette was even appropriate at that moment.

Many in society will take some convincing about this new way of dealing with death and grief, but this is how we communicate the minutiae of our lives today, so Facebook may be the most appropriate place when it comes to expressing something really important to those that matter.

The number of people who changed their profile pictures to ones of themselves and Josh was a silent but incredibly powerful statement. For all the scare stories about social networks eroding cultural values, they equally offer a very traditional form of support during difficult times. And if they make speaking about – and therefore coping with – death a little easier for us collectively then that is surely only a benefit to society, however we end up redrawing the lines of etiquette and media behaviour.

Tom had worked alongside Josh at one of London's major music venues, The Ministry of Sound. He wrote: *'The saddest thing is that such an enthusiastic proponent of all today's communications technologies will not now see them develop. RIP Josh.'*

For some, the rapid growth of social media, and the various platforms where we can show our friends just how exciting and enviable our lives are – pictures of our latest batch of sourdough bread, smiling selfies from the beach, that stunning view from our bedroom window – presents a disturbing juxtaposition between the mundane, mostly superficial but always transient nature of Facebook and Instagram and the enormity and permanence of death. It may be true that social media sites are poorly suited to the 'strangeness' of grief but they also make possible communities that rely on each other to explain the inexplicable, to help them understand our 'new normal'.

There is, of course, a difference between the more public and therefore more anonymous forums where grief in all its complexities is the easy appeal of platitudes – 'I'm so sorry for your loss', 'I can't imagine how it feels' – and more closed groups that find comfort from sharing their stories as well as their worries, their fears and often the exclusion they experience from friends and family. Such, for instance, are the portals provided by charities like The Compassionate Friends – peer-to-peer networks that operate on a physical person-to-person level but also, and crucially, online. Our own charity, The Good Grief Project, grew out of the work we did for TCF and is similarly embedded in social media. We wouldn't be able to join with others and share our knowledge and ideas as effectively or to receive the support necessary for true healing, without it. In times of lockdown occasioned by the Covid-19 pandemic and the isolation that we have all had to endure, social media has become even more important.

It started with the decision not to close Joshua's own Facebook account – a pretence, if you like,

that he is still out there somewhere in the ether. More than a decade later and with literally hundreds of posts that way outnumber his own (the last was a week before his accident – '8 January 2011: 7.2 million Vietnamese dong spent on a Honda Win = GAME ON') and the result is not only a continuing relationship with our son but an ongoing rapport with his 'friends'.

It is, of course, in those relationships that he now resides to the extent that they initiated the blog page 'Postcards to Josh'. Abroad when he died, the idea that friends would still send him postcards from their own travels might seem a little 'forced'. But whatever their beliefs, the idea that we can send messages to the dead addressing them in the present (Josh, we talk to YOU) confirms our attachment to him and to each other. Social media allows an illusion on many levels – imperfect but soothing.

We now have very active pages and groups across all social media. While the websites for the charity and our film work are important bases from which to promote our work, it's on Facebook, Instagram and Twitter that we conduct daily conversations with our 'community', now almost 5,000 strong. The Good Grief Photo Project, for instance, is a closed group that encourages a cross current of visual ideas that help its members develop ways of expressing their feelings that are less 'word' bound. Few will 'know' each other in real life, but we can dip in and out of forums on social media in the same way as our emotional energy waxes and wanes. Never before have the bereaved had such easy access to the means to share our grief beyond our own immediate environment. Instant and transient it may be, but grief is now more social, more open and possibly more radical, rebellious even, and that is a good thing.

alone or together | the value of sharing your story

To share or not to share the story of our grief? Some will want to keep their feelings private, to hold on to the memory of their loved one in a way that is perhaps undiluted by public expression. Others will find comfort in openly telling the story of the person's life and their death. Many people will oscillate between the two: sometimes it's good to talk, on other occasions we prefer to stay silent.

At some point, though – and this may not be well understood by those who have not suffered a significant loss – we will feel compelled to tell the story of our grief. Research shows that openly sharing one's story verbally has a cathartic or liberating effect that alleviates psychological distress.

Equally, writing about our grief either in diary form, as letters, as poetry or even just scribbled on the back of an envelope – maybe as a message to the deceased to be buried or burned as part of a ritual – all these actions will help make their death more real. The mere practice of writing will concentrate the mind for a moment in which we are completely connected with our loved one.

It's a truism that as humans we are bound to tell stories as a way of making sense of the world. Stories are an instinctive and deliberate attempt to convey purpose and meaning, especially when the meaning of our lives and of those we love has been shattered by a death or other significant trauma. If we understand the basics of what a story is, for instance, a narrative that contains characters and a plot that evolves over time, then we can see how they can capture emotional events and make connections with others who may or may not have different experience of those events.

The story may differ or evolve over time but a story told well will have a more meaningful impact if it connects the 'unknown to the known'. If good stories have a beginning, a middle and an end, then the listener will be made aware of things unknown to them before they heard it. Similarly, there is cathartic value in the way that the telling of a story, sometimes over and over again, will turn our own disbelief or disassociation (about our loss) into something more tangible, more believable, and in that sense more known. In the end the story we share will make us feel less alone.

19
Stronger than my love: Jessica Carmody Nathan

Jessica Carmody Nathan is an emerging talent in the UK folk scene, a singer/songwriter for whom the themes of love and loss have always featured strongly in her work. She is also a childhood friend of our Josh and we have close family ties with her parents. In 2019 Jess's dad Jack was diagnosed with pancreatic cancer and died within weeks. A year later she recorded My Jupiter, a collection of six songs all written since her father's death.

Writing songs about my life has always been something that occurs naturally. It is my way of distilling the complexities of the world. But commodifying grief feels unnatural; I've struggled with the dichotomy between the soul-making process of writing about life and the soul-taking process of trying to package that life (or death) so it is 'consumable'.

I want to say I have created something from my dad's death. I want to say I recognise and accept this stranger who I know only as a fatherless daughter.

When I began writing *My Jupiter*, I was subscribing to the notion that art can be therapeutic. I had just lost two grandparents in quick succession, and a few months later my dad was told he had pancreatic cancer and died within four weeks.

In this past year of writing, self-doubt, recording, crying, re-recording, pacing, mixing, note-making, listening, re-mixing and finally mastering, I find it hard to believe that this process has been helpful. That's not to say art can't be healing, but I'm certain that listening to my grief, over and over, does nothing to alleviate the weight of absence.

Jessica and Jack perform at Joshua's Funeral,
photo by Fred Chance
Far left: Jessica Nathan with her father Jack

Writing a song can teach you how you feel; it is the window to your gut, the telephone wire to your heart. These visceral mouthpieces have been hard to hear. I would not do it again, nor advise you to. But my friend did suggest that I might be helping my future self in ways I can't fathom or realise yet, which did console me a little. Except, this process has been like giving birth to a tyrannical monster with spikes and venom ready to incapacitate me at any moment.

Accepting that there is no end is the hardest part of grief. I'm told it gets better with time but, after a year, I am back where I started.

I am a strong believer in the well-traversed line that life and art imitate each other. All my songs now sound as if I've already lost my dad.

What I did not consider was how detached from the world I would feel. Past-life Carmody was earthed. I could write about loss because I had never experienced loss. I had never 'touched grief's core', as the Nigerian writer, Chimamanda Ngozi Adichie describes it. Carmody without her father was Carmody without her lyrics. My ability to find the language for the inexpressible had vanished. This grief was too colossal to be packed into a song. It was, and is, ineffable and I still cannot grasp it.

This record was an attempt to write cohesively about an absence I have not yet accepted. It came from my need to document the past year, no matter how difficult, or treacherous, it became.

Stronger than my love

There was a war
between your sickness and me
and it turns out all my lines were prophecies
she calls me to the bedroom says she
hears you in another bird's song
plug in electric candles
that's how we reach you now you're gone

And how, how can this be stronger than my love?
And how, how can this be stronger than my love?
Than my love

We kept hope
'cause we needed to believe
without you I'm reborn I'm a baby in the bluest
world I've ever seen
and it's just like Lewis wrote your absence is
like the sky spread over everything
but I know I'll always hear you
In every note I'll ever sing

And how, how can this be stronger than my love?
And how, how can this be stronger than my love?
Than my love
Than my love
Than my love

That's where this song came from – love.
It came from watching my dad deteriorate day by
day regardless of the curries, the prayers, the
alternative medicines, and the fervent research.
One morning I was sitting by his bedside watching
him drift in and out of consciousness and I
thought, how can cancer be stronger than our love?
It sounds bizarre that I thought of a lyric while he
was dying. Worse still, I thought of a hook. But
that is the beauty of song writing: you can't control
when, or how, it comes to you. I wanted to hear
and accept the idea that was given to me, no
matter how painful. Though, what was further
problematic was accepting that my dad's demise
had become my muse. Previously I had no qualms
writing autobiographically, but this act of creation
felt sinful, but necessary.

A year in, the inexplicable swings of euphoria have
faded and there is little interest in my 'new life'. I
have noticed incremental changes but, at such a
cost, I was anticipating some sort of
enlightenment. This idea feels laughable, to
assume transformation from loss. But I am still
searching for my 'new earth', because without it
there is just absence, and it stains everything.
Spring days, swimming in the sea, chocolate
dessert, music. It all feels coloured by the fact he
isn't here. This is the reason I included the line by
C.S. Lewis 'your absence is like the sky, spread
over everything', as it is beautiful and accurate.
The loss of the person you love is like the sky,
dictating the light and shadows below.

My Jupiter

My Jupiter
Where did you go?
unimaginable
empty space

My Jupiter
I would orbit around you
built a self that I knew
I cannot trace

And I, oh I, I oh I
bear the unbearable without you

My Jupiter
I cannot fathom it here
it's like you've disappeared
some place I cannot name

My Jupiter
can't conjure you in my dreams
can't make out those childhood scenes
that wrote my days

And I, oh I, I oh I
bear the unbearable without you

And I, oh I, I oh I
bear the unbearable without you

Jessica plays at the Ministry of Sound where Josh used to work, photomontage by Jimmy Edmonds

I started writing 'My Jupiter' in December, a few months after my dad died. It was inspired by Ian, a psychotherapist and astrologer who offered to do our charts. Ian spoke a lot about my dad's Jupitarian energy. Dad was the embodiment of life. He loved to fill the room and talk to anyone and everyone he could. He was wide-eyed with a passion for the world and all its elements. Never afraid of difficult conversations, never worrying about making people uncomfortable, never stopping until he had uncovered something in them. Throughout my life I have let this energy carry me. His vibrancy made me friends on family holidays, encouraged me to go for opportunities at school and, most importantly, led me to continue in a music career that I so often found debilitating.

When he was dying, I decided to voice-note some of our conversations. I can't emphasise enough how grateful I am to have these, and I would absolutely recommend it to anyone in a similar position. I often felt like he was the one fuelling my confidence and drive and I wasn't sure whether I would be able to access these parts of me without him. His response was the best, most dad-like answer he could have given: he told me to 'internalise the good object'. To take all his passion for my music and try to own, accept and nurture it, to allow it to be a part of me. Because, after all, he is part of me, whether he is here or not.

My Jupiter is published by Young Poet Records.

20
An active grief:
Jimmy Edmonds and Jane Harris

'**G**rief is energy,' said Maria Mascarucci. She had been dealing with grief for many years before joining us on our first residential weekend retreat for bereaved parents and siblings. The mother of three stillborn children, she was looking for a way to channel that energy more creatively. Our own understanding of grief is that almost by definition it is a creative process – one of doing and creating new things that fill the void left by a loved one's absence, things that would and could not have existed before and unless they had died. Over the course of the weekend Maria, along with 25 others, took part in three different workshops all carefully designed to help the bereaved find a more proactive way of managing and expressing their grief.

Soon after Josh had died, we recognised the need to be more creative in the way we dealt with our grief. To move forward (as opposed to moving on)

in our grief we needed to be more purposeful, more active, more energetic. To quote the title of Gary Andrews' book, if we want to 'find joy' again we needed to become intentional grievers, not victims of its circumstance.

People talk of the 'push me – pull you' of grief – alternating moments of reflection and repair, and that sooner or later the need to rebuild a life will become more dominant, necessary, essential even, if we are to properly respect our dead and live the life they would want us to. We had emerged from that early dense fog of grief in which we were just going through the motions and were now beginning to look forward as much as we were looking back. Along with the discovery that to laugh and smile was not to dishonour Josh, we had realised that we could no longer rely purely on memories to get us through the day – especially as they became more and more distant.

Early morning moment on our Active Grief Weekend

As a family we had also realised that being open with our grief and finding opportunities to share it was so, so healing. We all had different skills that we could bring to the table that then became the Active Grief Programme: Jimmy leads a photography workshop; Jane brought her therapeutic skills to these and the mindfulness practice that runs throughout the weekend; Josh's brother Joe (a personal trainer) delivers the 'active' physical exercise sessions; and close friend Jo Bousfield, a community theatre director whose daughter Harrie died at around the same time as Josh, runs a course on creative writing. To complete the picture, Josh's younger sister Rosa brings her skills as an amateur chef to provide all the meals for our guests.

At the time of writing, we have now held seven such weekends, providing support and encouragement to around 150 bereaved parents and half a dozen siblings. Held in remote rural locations, they are similar to a yoga or therapeutic retreat, save that these are exclusively for members of families bereaved after the death of a son or daughter. And it matters not how old the child was, or how or when they died. What is important is that we share a common grief, and our learnings from that grief. The Active Grief Weekends are modest and intimate, more informal. This also adds to the sense of safety that our 'guests' experience and the chance to freely explore ways to express their grief in company with others who they know 'get it'.

It takes some nerve to come on such a weekend – to have to face a lot of other bereaved parents and all the emotions that they will bring up. We know that. It was a good two years before Jimmy could give thought to other people's stories of grief – it's too much of a burden when everything is still so painful, so raw. To take that first step and fill out one of our registration forms is then an important,

relationships

Perhaps more than any other bereavement, the death of a child has a profound impact on our relationships with others, particularly our life partners. Rocked by grief, many couples find that sharing their true feelings could jeopardise their relationship or even lead to it breaking down completely. For others it may bring them closer, but for our grief to be resolved in a healthy and life-affirming way, we do need to have some understanding of the way parents will grieve differently.

We know that the birth of a child makes a big difference to the way we relate to our partners. Becoming a parent changes things. No surprise, then, that their death will affect the way we grieve, both as individuals and as a couple.

Although men and women grieve differently, all couples and close loving relationships will or can find a real disparity in their responses to the trauma of their child's death.

When we find grief is too overwhelming, we can become preoccupied with our own feelings, or we internalise them as a way of shielding our partner from its intensity. The risk of misunderstanding is ever present – as we cope with our own feelings along with all the everyday demands of living, work and other children, it's easy to feel distant from one another or shut out. This can lead to extreme or atypical behaviour, resentment and division, especially if one partner seems to be functioning or coping better than the other.

On the other hand, we might allow ourselves to grieve fully only when we are sure our partner is ok. But it's important to recognise all the heightened emotions that come with grief: guilt, shame, anger and blame are difficult emotions that we may find we have very differing capacities to handle.

Seeing our partner in pain is hard to bear, revealing our own pain is hard to do. But masking our grief can be problematic, in the sense that it can give the impression we are in control and so leave ourselves without the support we could be getting from our partner.

Much of our own response to tragedy is determined by our family and cultural background. Our own parents were our first teachers, but there may also be unresolved losses in our background that our partner may or may not have known about that will inevitably make our current grief more intense. Not recognising our different ways of grieving can add to a further layer of grief. Good communication, then, is the key. It helps not to evaluate or judge our partner's behaviour, to instead try to see things through their eyes, to have fewer expectations and learn to forgive. Notice how in grief our focus will shift from dwelling on the loss to a need to find respite from the pain, and that we will necessarily do this in tandem with one another. We have found that setting aside regular times to talk to each other when we won't be disturbed is important. If things remain difficult there is no shame in seeking out professional help with a relationship counsellor.

intentional and resolute act. We honour that courage, in that it confirms our own now proactive approach.

All the 'work' we do on the retreats flows from the concept of continuing the bond with the deceased, of not wanting to cut off from them but of building

a new kind of relationship with them, and of finding ways to integrate our loss into our lives. This is not passive work, but requires the active intent of the participants. We make it clear that there is no compulsion to join in any of the sessions but not to do so would be to miss out on

Left: Active Grief session, photo Lizzie Pickering
Above: Maria Mascarucci, photo Rosa Harris Edmonds
Below: Active Grief session, photo Lizzie Pickering

an important encounter with your true feelings. Whether we are making new photographs, writing short stories or allowing ourselves to become truly physical in the expression of our grief, we are necessarily spending time with our child and giving focused attention to our loss and what it means for us in an almost primal and manifestly visceral way.

'When Joe allowed me to really let rip – oh, that felt so good. It's done more for me in the sixteen months since I lost Alex than anything.' Poppy Hocken's son had taken his own life, and this was the first time she had truly and confidently confronted the pain of her loss in any kind of a public way, during a boxercise session.

In a way, that's the key. Engaging with both the physical and the mental aspect of grief allows for a fuller expression of our feelings. If playing with words 'unleashed my sadness,' one mum told us,

the boxing 'unleashed my anger'.

Meeting and talking with other bereaved families is an important aspect of the weekends. We eat and we talk, we relax in company we can trust. We're in a bubble, safe from that other world where life goes on as normal. We learn from each other and go away feeling that we understand our own grief better, that we have found meaning in our sorrow, and we can better weave the reality of our loss into our daily lives.

There's clearly been a shift in recent years in the way we understand grief and the impact it has on us both as individuals and as a society. Theories of how people heal after a significant trauma or the death of a loved one have considerably advanced our knowledge of what it means to grieve. Seeing this emotion as energy, energy that we engage with proactively, is perhaps a slightly more nuanced way of understanding how we can process our grief.

From our perspective and from our experience, active grieving is essential for our survival. It allows us to grieve outside the box, and to lament without shame. An intentional grief is a creative grief, one that we can take pride in and one that enables us to fully live with our loss.

101

'Those who will not slip beneath
the still surface on the well of grief

turning downward through its black water
to the place we cannot breathe

will never know the source from which we drink,
the secret water, cold and clear,

nor find in the darkness glimmering
the small round coins
thrown by those who wished for something else.'

David Whyte, The Well of Grief

21
Secret waters: Jimmy Edmonds

I have always enjoyed a good swim, whether in a pool or open water. But since Josh died I have taken to swimming with added enthusiasm, especially wild, open and, yes, cold-water swimming.

Grief and cold water, very cold water, do have a lot in common, mostly in the sense of being alien environments that one would not normally choose to enter. In winter the temperatures of our rivers and lakes (in the UK) can drop to well under 5°C, though sea temperatures average out at around 10°C. (For comparison, most pools are kept at 25–30°C and our normal body temperature is 37°C.)

So what's the attraction? What does swimming in cold waters do for me? The answer is that it connects me to Josh in ways that I have found to be both surprising and rewarding. Whyte's poem is a metaphor, but it could equally describe reality. In both senses, swimming in those dark waters

has revealed and is still revealing much that I would not have had to confront had Josh not died. I can safely say that without my swimming I don't think I would be grieving so well – though putting into words just how is not going to be easy. As a journey it's so much about feelings and a visceral experience that takes you to a place where words and metaphors are rendered redundant.

My first dip into the cold – my first intentional dip, one with Josh very much on my mind – was in forbidden waters. There are signs all around a lake where we used to live declaring 'NO SWIMMING!' but it was here that Josh used to come with his friends on a sunny summer afternoon. I had not known this at the time. It was his younger sister, Rosa, who told me, as together we walked through the autumnal woods to find what must be one of the most delightful swim spots in the county, if not the whole universe. The lake is deep, very deep, and bordered by mixed

deciduous woods that descend right to the water's edge. There's a fallen tree trunk (big enough to show up on Google Maps) on which you can climb out and launch yourself into the lake's silky brown waters, something that Josh would've done many a time. Again, I did not know this, so my introduction to nature's very own watery pleasures was accompanied with a renewed sense of getting to know him in a way that began to put a bit more substance into my relationship with him – to begin to fill the void left by his absence.

I have now swum there in all seasons and all weathers. In summer, when the sun warms us, there's no problem finding companions; in winter, in the wind and rain, I mostly go alone.

To swim alone, I have found, is to be closer to the well that is my grief.

Extract from my swim log
Thursday 9 Oct 2017, Local lake
(water temp: 7°C)

It's raining and I hesitate a little before getting into the car. The walk on arrival takes me from a single track lane (no parking here!) through the gate marked private and then to the locked gate (which today is open). Autumn is here and the track through the woods is thickly covered with brown and yellow leaves – wet and soggy and on their way to the next cycle of nature's work.

I slide into the water easily and feel the squidge between my toes, then find that small platform of wood that acts as a stepping stone for the way out. Two good spurts of front crawl to the fallen tree and back then I try some breaststroke. My BS (breaststroke) is crap but the wind has got up and is sending sheets of rain and spray along the lake surface, so I breast into it, sinking deep and rising as high as I can – it's magic, like being the figurehead on the bow of a ship. I love the water now – the emptiness of it, feeling the rain on my face, seeing my arms stretching ahead in the green-brown gloom – upside-down raindrops on the lake surface like polyps, hundreds and thousands of mini stalagmites popping up dead centre of a glistening ripple. They mirror in a slightly larger way, the pins and needles that are pricking me all over. I spin again, giving a good kick to raise some froth, then front crawl into the cold, cold void.

Back on the bank I stand awhile, totally naked, and feel very comfortable with my aloneness. All the time I wish it was not so, but the death of Joshua has produced a solitary moment right in the heart of me that has found a place right here.

In the last few years small groups and networks of people wanting to explore the joys of outdoor swimming have sprung up worldwide, along with all the attendant Facebook groups and websites and press interest.

Our contributors Ruth Fitzmaurice, Billie Oliver and Sophie Pearce, have all found companionship in this tribe of open-water swimmers, and each and every one of them will attest to the benefits of swimming with a social group. By meeting at regular times, not just to swim together but to chat and encourage one another, they argue that belonging to a like-minded group of friends mitigates the social isolation often felt by the bereaved. Membership of such groups is very informal, but somehow even the loosest of bonds with those who maybe have similar stories of

the physical effects of grief

Grief is not an illness but a normal, natural healing response to a loss of any kind, yet it can affect the body in surprising ways. Commonly, bereaved people report feeling exhaustion, loss of appetite, sleeplessness, recurring headaches, as well as a literal and very real heartache. Intense grief can also increase blood pressure, with the risk of blood clots, respiratory problems including shortness of breath and asthma, along with other stomach and gut problems. It is perhaps no coincidence that our physical organs, such as the heart, lungs and kidneys, share a common language with our emotional responses, including love, fear and anger. Over the long term, grief can impact on every part of the human body, including the endocrine and immune systems – a complex network of glands and organs that control the release of hormones that coordinate our body's metabolism, energy levels and response to injury, stress and mood.

Getting active can help
We all know that exercise is good for you. It helps with weight loss, cholesterol, blood pressure, energy levels and more, but how does that work for the bereaved? Here's a brief explanation.

People struggling with low moods like depression, anxiety and other psychological disorders will have lower baselines of serotonin, one of two neurotransmitters released in our brain that help us feel happy and ok in the world. It stands to reason that these feel-good transmitters will suffer when tragedy and grief overcome us.

If one of the reasons we humans love food and alcohol is that they boost our serotonin levels, physical exercise will achieve the same effect but without the subsequent weight gain! At the same time, chemicals known as

Early morning at Cotswold Water Park

trauma and loss will help promote 'feelings of greater wellbeing and resilience'. You could call it peer pressure, but the 'tribe' keeps you keeping on. And cold water seems to bring the community even closer together.

I joined a bunch of guys at an inland lake in the Cotswolds – we formed a WhatsApp group called the Chilly Willies and made rude jokes that took the edge off the pain as we entered those icy waters. While I was the only bereaved parent in the group

endorphins are released in our body when we experience stress and, as we know, exercise is a form of stress – good stress as opposed to bad stress. These endorphins trigger the opiate receptors in our brains that both reduce our perception of pain and induce positive feelings similar to the effects of morphine and heroin but without their addictive qualities.

So far so good. How do I get off the couch to get all those feel-good juices flowing? Regular visits to the gym might seem a tad intimidating. The good news is that research shows that rather than 10-kilometre runs or working hard every other day weightlifting, a little-to-moderate daily exercise (say 20–30 minutes) is actually better for boosting the mood. Additionally, regular exercise helps facilitate rest and sleep, which can be elusive in early grief. Keep in mind that some exercise is better than none. A simple brisk walk requires no

equipment, is cost-effective and easy to achieve. Whatever your choice – cycling, jogging, dancing, aerobics, swimming – our advice is to take it gently to start with before gradually increasing the effort. And find someone to exercise with, a partner or a friend. Mutual encouragement will bring emotional comfort, too.

In summary, this long and difficult journey called grief is manifested in symptoms that result from the connection between the mind and body. Careful attention to health issues during bereavement can help relieve some of the normal grief responses and, more importantly, prevent a worsening of existing disease conditions and prevent future health problems.

Exercise cannot extinguish grief, but it can play a valuable role in helping people adapt to loss.

Closer to the well that is my grief, photomontage Jimmy Edmonds

the others all had a history of some kind of mental health issue, even if this wasn't necessarily their prime motivation for joining us. We've done night swims, sunrise swims, swims through the ice, and swims where no one has said a word.

Saturday 29 September, 6am, Lake 32, Cotswold Water Park (water temp: 15°C)

To swim at this hour is almost bliss, to swim with these two is life-affirming. Three men in a lake – to turn and find the moon still hanging in the sky. This is play time more than swim time; John tries his double-arm backstroke, I keep to the front crawl side by side with Donny. We stop, admire, laugh and swim on round the island and back to the first pink buoy, by now lost in the rising mist. At this hour the lake, its light and its air, changes by the minute – cold water is no threat, purely a stimulus to the life force, adrenaline for the stroke, a comfort blanket from which to enjoy nature's glory.

For bereaved parent Billie Oliver (see page 114), swimming has helped her to not only navigate but survive 'those stormy waters of grief'. She explains, 'There is a sense of group achievement and camaraderie, and always after a cold-water swim, lots and lots of laughter. It is impossible, I have found, to complete a cold-water swim without a big smile on your face.'

Sally Goble is addicted. 'The friends you meet in cold water,' she says, 'are the best. Cold-water swimmers are adventurous, full of life and quick to laugh. They sparkle like the icy water they inhabit.'

Friday 2 February, Branscombe, Devon (water temp: 9°C)

A gloriously sunny day and a walk along the cliff tops to Beer and back. Then for a dip in the sea. The tide is out and the sea is unruffled, salty and friendly. I swim out 25 metres or so from the shore. The numbness sets in but I feel at home and comfortable –
to be in the water, swimming and stroking my way through its envelope of calm and finding

a peace that is both active and restful, discovering
a source of physical pain that
I can handle, that I can reside in, that will in some
way equate with this unknowing about Josh's
death. No one, I suspect, can give you
a straightforward answer to why they swim
in cold waters – they will try to explain but reason
will never reveal what it means to live on in the
aftermath of death.

In recent years there has been a huge amount
of scientific research and mounting evidence for
what many would call the 'bleeding obvious' – that
immersion in cold water is good for the soul. While
we are variously described as mad fools, totally
bonkers or just plain crazy, bathing in sea, rivers
and lakes has been part of human existence long
before the construction of the municipal lido or
swimming pool. Moreover, the curative and
therapeutic value of sea-bathing in the colder
winter months has been meticulously studied since
Victorian times. In a recent article Billie Oliver
quotes Wallace Nichols from his book *Blue Mind*:

'...when we step into the water, our cortisol levels
drop and our brains switch into a different mode.'

Nichols asserts that this can boost creativity,
settle the brain and the body down and reduce
stress and reconnects you to the place, to yourself
and to those you are with – and makes you happy.
That immersion in cold water can have an anti-
inflammatory effect on both physical and mental

conditions is further explored by a Finnish group
of researchers who found that not only does
exposure to open skies help us to feel better, but
the authors reported how cold-water swimming
induces a stress reaction, activating the
sympathetic nervous system and increasing
the secretion of hormones that influence mood.
They concluded that this is probably one factor
behind the refreshing and pain-relieving effect
of winter swimming.

Now when it comes to grief, this feels to me
somewhat contradictory. While the restorative
effect of being in nature is so welcome, it's the
physical pain and the unease that comes from
being in an alien environment that I actually
crave. I do not want the pain of my grief to be so
relieved. I need to come to terms with the fear of
the unknown – of those dark waters – but I don't
need to not be afraid.

**Sunday 4 February, Branscombe, Devon
(water temp: 9°C)**

I turn and head out to sea – out to the vastness of
the ocean – such a different light now – sparkling
dark – what joy to just spin around in this
saltiness. The water will hold me, comfort me, it
will not let me go, and I trust the sea and I trust
myself more and more each time. Again, it feels
like this is a journey really worth travelling – to
find the unknown in this coldness, to find
whatever is there for my body as it seeks more

'As I get into the rhythm of my swim, stroke after stroke, breath after breath, I can achieve a kind of serenity – there's a peace here, where alone in this watery world I feel I am as close to death as I dare go and as close to Josh as I'll ever be while I still breathe.'

and more cold, to be frozen and yet not frozen because I still have a heart that beats. Turning again to the shore with the sun behind me, I reach out and swim with the waves and within minutes I'm thrown up onto the beach, crunching my foot against some rock – grrr...!! The animal sea has made sure I don't forget her.

To swim alone...
The companionship of other swimmers is life-affirming. Let's say being in the water with other 'hydrophiles' is good for the soul, but for me swimming itself is essentially a solitary activity. You can run or ride with buddies and still hold a conversation together, they are sociable activities. People do swim and chat together but it's likely they'll be doing breaststroke and taking in the scenery at the same time. I do front crawl so my head and my airways are for the most part underwater. And I like it like that. I love being on my own underwater, feeling the water gliding past me as I pull on each stroke, breathing on every fourth and finding the rhythm that will take me to the 'zone'. There is no other activity that I have

found that is so meditative, so in the moment and so far away from reality or the timescale of everyday living.

Saturday 19 January, Branscombe, Devon
There is no time here – more accurately, I am in geological time, where there are no hours or minutes or seconds – just the neverending tide and a billion years of rock strata, all the product of the rise and fall of this stuff I am swimming in. I am less than a speck.

Sophie Pierce describes how in the water she is 'paused in a liminal space' that mirrors the strange world in which she found herself after her son Felix's death.

Cold water especially produces a sharp bodily response, 'like a re-set button', which connects her 'with the elements, with life itself, in an unmediated way.'

I too have found that space. Space that is thinking time, but more importantly feeling time. And what

Photo Jane Harris

I'm feeling is, firstly, a mild elation that I'm in a supportive environment (in water mostly you float). Secondly, a degree of fear that the environment is not necessarily safe (you can drown). Thirdly, a sense of wonder. In water, especially open water, I am in another world, a world that is full of life (on the lake we have swans, cormorants, geese, moorhens, carp, and I've seen pike and crayfish, too…). It is a world in which is it easy to imagine you are flying. The bottom of the lake is like a new landscape, changing with the seasons, as it drifts slowly beneath me.

Fourth, and this might seem dramatic, but as I get into the rhythm of my swim, stroke after stroke, breath after breath, I achieve a kind of serenity – there's a peace here. Alone in this watery world I feel I am as close to death as I dare go and as close to Josh as I'll ever be while I still breathe.

a note about safety

Cold-water swimming is not without risks. To be able to swim safely in temperatures below 10°C, it is best to undergo a gradual acclimatisation process. Ideally, you should have been swimming throughout the summer and slowly working down the temperature scale as it naturally drops. This will help you get to know how your body reacts to the cold. Everyone responds differently to cold-water immersion, so it's important that you listen to and understand your body. It's not a competition. The key points are: acclimatise; be visible; know your limits; warm up gradually; and unless you are totally sure of the risks, never swim alone. Finally, if you have hypertension, a heart condition or have ever had cold-induced asthma, it is advisable to check with your doctor first.

The Outdoor Swimming Society provides excellent online resources and advice on acclimatisation and staying safe in open water:
www.outdoorswimmingsociety.com

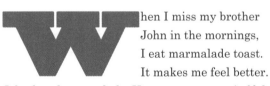

22
Sea soul: Ruth Fitzmaurice

Ruth Fitzmaurice is the author of
I Found My Tribe, *a memoir about life with her husband Simon, who died in 2017 almost a decade after being diagnosed with motor neurone disease. The book celebrates friendship and the curative power of swimming in all seasons. Ruth lives with her five children in Co Wicklow.*

Above right: Ruth prepares to swim, Ladies Cove Greystones, co Wicklow – 'It's the first time every time', photo Niall Meehan, Sea Studio
Above: Ruth Fitzmaurice, photo courtesy Sophie Hicks Agency

When I miss my brother John in the mornings, I eat marmalade toast. It makes me feel better. John loved marmalade. He was a proper mindful Paddington Bear. In 2019, aged 46, within a year and a half of his diagnosis, he died of a fast-growing, aggressive brain tumour. Two years before that, in 2017, my husband Simon died of motor neurone disease (MND) at the age of 43. He lived with MND for nine years and could not move or breathe for most of it.

These are the facts as they happened. The above litany of loss gives me every reason to look for sympathy, remain broken and miserable, or feel robbed and landed with a raw deal. What if I told you I feel lucky and blessed? Not that they died, but for the lessons that so much loss has gifted me. You might wonder if I am a Jesus freak, or a kook, or a liar, or trying to promote some kind of new fad yoga practice or energy drink. Tell me to get lost. I

might do the same had I not been through it myself. I am less cynical. I am lucky.

When we drive by the ocean and streaks of sunlight spill through the clouds in every direction, I call them God's fingers and shout 'Look!' to my five children, 'Dadda is saying hello!' We hug trees when they miss him, because he loved forests. We eat Jaffa Cakes on his birthday and they beg me to tell them again and again how he could eat a whole pack at a time without stopping. His legacy lingers in the fabric of our daily lives, in the particular way my son bites his tongue when concentrating, or the blue shape of my daughter's eyes. In our unhealthy love for Jaffa Cakes.

Why am I lucky? Because loss woke me to the fact that I am alive at all.

For months after he died, my husband lived in the floor-to-ceiling bookshelves he had loved and built in our kitchen. Here I could talk to him directly,

between remembered poems, scraps of paper and spidery handwriting scrawled in book margins. Most days I would say, 'Simon, give me something,' then glean the book spines and choose one jutting out further than the rest. Often, we still talk to each other this way.

Simon lived with MND for almost a decade. His was a powerful flame extinguished by degrees, by ventilators, by round-the-clock nurses, eye-gaze technology and a computerised voice. This prolonged loss was too much and it brought me to nature. I took up sea swimming and plunged myself year-round into the freezing Irish sea, ridding my mind of the painful chatter. Sea swimming lifted the daily sadness from my bones. I emerged every day lighter, a clean slate, until the very next day, when sadness weighed me down again.

You can embrace the seasons, make your peace with the life–death–life cycle, grapple with acceptance, but to experience such active loss is

debilitating. The body experiences trauma and it doesn't forget. Grief takes you down and immobilises you. It leaves you with very large, visible holes. What is needed then is a full keening, a wailing and gnashing of teeth, an existential scream that shakes the world. This is what is supposed to happen if you have ever loved at all.

Swimming stopped the grief chatter. It emptied my head as I begged the cold ocean for that elusive thing called ease and long-forgotten silences. With a clear head, that's when it happened. Among the waves, along the shore, between treasure pockets of glinting sea glass, flocks of birds swooping overhead and glimpses of the fleeting sunrise, I heard the beautiful sounds and rhythms of nature. It was nothing less than the music of my own soul.

I am my words and my soul is me

Grief was a rude awakening. It woke me to the fact I have a soul. A soul is harder to ignore when it is screaming. There is nothing pleasant about it, but you gain a new alertness. A soul in pain is a soul that has woken up. It is not for the fainthearted. I discovered that my heart is huge and my love infinite. It stirred up my creative energy, because I had no choice but to write my way out of this. I wrote like a maniac and realised my words had a beat to them too, much like a song. The soul is our own inner landscape and its natural rhythms are as musical and breathtaking as the biggest view. I am my words and my soul is me.

I swam and wrote about it and the book took on a life of its own. People listened and could relate. This brought enormous comfort and my song got stronger. A whole orchestra swelled.

Above: photo Niall Meehan, Sea Studio
Left: Ruth with her tribe, photo Alison Mckenny

What is grief? Only the small matter of finding your soul's song and connecting to others. Only the most intense human experience we can have. In my own small blip of existence, I have learned more about life through walking with death than anything else. Now each day I make a promise to my dear departed brother and husband. Life is a precious gift. I promise them I will try to live well. I thank them for the lessons and tell them I miss them. Sometimes I cry. Often I swim. None of us will live forever. I hug my children tighter, eat marmalade toast and the odd Jaffa Cake, talk to my bookshelf, read poetry, attempt yoga poses, sample the latest energy drink, continue to create, laugh and sing. In this beautiful short life, I walk on with love.

I Found My Tribe, Ruth Fitzmaurice
(Chatto & Windus, 2017)

23
Just keep swimming:
Billie Oliver

Billie Oliver is a Visiting Research Fellow with the Centre for Public Health and Wellbeing at the University of the West of England, Bristol. She was first introduced to open-water swimming in 2015, following the sudden and traumatic death of her daughter Wendy.

When people learn that I am an all-year-round sea swimmer, the most common question they ask – generally after they have made negative insinuations about the state of my mental health – is: why do you do it? There is no straightforward or simple answer to this question. My motivations have varied at different times along my journey. As a general response, however, I would say – in common with most other people I swim with – that I do it for my mental health and wellbeing.

My daughter, Wendy, died from suicide in June 2015. She was an active, beautiful, inspiring,

popular and creative young woman. The shock of her death and the loss of such a vibrant young woman sent waves through the community. As her parents we were confronted not only by our own grief, but by that of all those other people who had loved her.

As a personal trainer, Wendy had encouraged people to find new challenges, to be active and, more importantly, to have fun while doing it. Earlier in the year she had 'encouraged' a number of her clients to enter a 'fun' team triathlon that was due to take place in September 2015 – as it happens on the same date as what would have been her 35th birthday. After she died, it felt important to not only encourage every one of them to continue to take part, but for our family to enter a couple of teams as well. We needed an outlet for the powerful wave of grief and loss that we were experiencing and also to feel part of something that she was involved with – to continue her legacy. I discovered that being a part of that lovely, fun group of people who all loved Wendy was a wonderful, warm, holding, healing and important experience for me. And it was through doing that event that I discovered the healing power of sea swimming.

Top and far left: Billie Oliver. Left: Wendy Oliver

I had never swum in anything other than calm waters before, and it is no understatement to say that on that first occasion, walking into the decidedly choppy, uncertain and definitely chilly waters of the Severn Estuary, I found it to be one of the most difficult and terrifying experiences of my life. With bursting lungs and doubting my ability to go on, an enormous sob that had been building up inside me was released and I cried freely and cathartically into my goggles. It felt to me, as I floundered my way through the waves, that she was beside me, cheering me on, willing me to keep going – and beaming with pride when I completed it.

Taking up open-water swimming offered me a challenge, a purpose and something to focus on when grief threatened to overwhelm me. Grief, I have found, is a bit like the sea: it comes in waves. Like the tides, it comes and goes. Sometimes the waves are small and gentle, predictable and manageable. At other times they knock you right over when you least expect it. I discovered that the sea, with its vastness, its majesty and power, its rhythm and flow, has the ability to heal and to soothe me.

In the depth of my grief, I found that the sea was in tune with my grief, which at those times felt like anxiety, like a panic attack. These are the times when I just needed to keep swimming. I now swim in the sea all year round. I have frequently found that in the warmer, summer months the sea can be comforting, enveloping, supportive and soothing. In the colder winter months, when only shorter swims are feasible, the shock of entering the icy water instantly erases any painful thoughts and feelings. The cold water quietens the mind, washes away the butterflies and leads to a sense of achievement, of overcoming something – and of surviving.

'Just keep swimming' became my mantra as I worked through days, months – and now years – since Wendy died. Swimming in the sea has inspired me to write – about grief, about fear and about hope. I find that writing about these reflections helps me to make sense of the complex range of emotions that I continue to experience. My daughter Wendy was also a creative, artistic and poetic young woman who loved music, and so when I am thinking about what I am going to write, I try to shape it around the words that inspire me – and inspired her – in literature, poetry and lyrics. It is one more way of keeping her close to me and of involving her in my swimming journey.

24
To breathe again: Jane Harris and Jimmy Edmonds

he first time I laughed, I thought what a horrible person I was to laugh when my child had died. I didn't want to enjoy anything or eat the food he liked because he couldn't do it.' So says bereaved mother Denise in our film *A Love That Never Dies*. Her son Nicholas had died ten years earlier from an accidental drug overdose.

Our son Josh also died over ten years ago and that fear that we would somehow be dishonouring his memory should we start enjoying life again still haunts us... but not as badly as it used to. In fact, to smile, to laugh, to enjoy good food, to dance

even, having fun has become essential to the way we now live our lives – to our grief.

This is not to say that we have 'moved on' from Josh's death, that we have got over his not being here – not at all. But in the same way that our lungs still breathe and our hearts still pump blood through our veins, we cannot help but engage with life and all that it throws at us, the good and the bad.

This is the definition of grief for us, something we like to share as the general ethos for all our work for The Good Grief Project. Grief is not about hiding away in a darkened room (though we've

post-traumatic growth

'When we are no longer able to change a situation, we are challenged to change ourselves.'

Viktor Frankl, *Man's Search for Meaning*

Following trauma, we look for stability. The world we knew is changed and meaning has gone out of our lives. Initially, there is nothing to be done. We are overcome with despair. Nothing works. We don't even want to think about finding a solution.

When you talk to people in the early stages of grief, they often believe they won't get through it. We felt this at the beginning of our own grief, but sometimes you have to have your back against the wall before you can move forward. The complex reality is that while there's a huge part of us that wants to keep things as they were, we also crave change – because in the end we recognise that we have been changed, in the most fundamental way.

Post-traumatic growth is often confused with 'resilience', but the two are quite different. While resilience can be seen as a personal characteristic, with the ability to bounce back and regain a sense of normality, growth after trauma occurs when a less resilient person finds their fundamental belief system has been rocked to the core, forcing them to challenge their original world view. For the bereaved this may be hard, relentless work involving much distress and confusion as we try to understand why such a terrible thing has happened, but for Richard Tedeschi and Lawrence Calhoun, who coined the term 'post-traumatic growth', there are seven areas of growth that can spring from adversity:

- Greater appreciation of life
- Greater appreciation and strengthening of close relationships
- Increased compassion and altruism
- The identification of new possibilities or purpose in life
- Greater awareness of and utilisation of personal strengths
- Enhanced spiritual development
- Creative growth

While we can all recognise that emotions like sadness, anger and anxiety are common responses to trauma, avoiding thoughts and feelings out of fear and denial can paradoxically make it worse, reinforcing our belief that the world really is unsafe. By bottling up our feelings in grief we are more likely to suffer physical or psychological symptoms, panic attacks, gut ache and lethargy, to name but a few. We then miss out on opportunities to recreate meaning and new and positive experiences. By opening up to and embracing our fears it is possible to face the world again with a deeper sense of meaning than we ever had before.

often done that), it's not endless days full of sadness and despair (even if at times it feels just that), it's not about being pissed off with a world that avoids talking about your child (that too), neither is it a pretence that you are holding everything together, that you have all the positive energy and emotional strength to see this shit out (again, we've faked it loads).

Neither is grief a passing phase, a moment of doom and gloom from which we will eventually emerge to the sunlit uplands of a happier and more productive life. No, grief is a condition, neither light nor dark. It's an ongoing, lifelong condition in which the first steps are about learning to accept that painful experience (including and especially the trauma of a child's death) is integral to our new reality, to a new way of living.

Since our son Josh died we have found sharing the story of our own grief with the photos and films we have made not only validate feelings that had initially seemed unwelcome in the world, they give sustenance to a new and ongoing relationship with him. By creating new work, work that did not exist before he died, work that can be viewed or read by others, we are speaking of Josh in ways that acknowledge that new relationship not only with him, but with all those who knew him and, importantly, many that didn't.

In our view, we cannot, nor should we, disconnect from all the difficult, brutal emotions that accompany grief. If we disconnect with the pain of our loss, we disconnect from the love we have for our child and the memories in which they have played such an important role. These are our history. They have made us who we are and who we have now become. Deny them and we deny ourselves the wisdom that grief can offer.

Similarly, if we deny ourselves fun, laughter and joy we do a disservice to our grief. Our loved ones would not want us to lead a miserable life – this is a common refrain but difficult to achieve, often undermined by the guilt that Denise alludes to in our film. Or is it fear? Fear of being accused of not grieving enough, that we don't miss them enough, haven't loved them enough, that we haven't been a good enough parent to them even and especially after they have died.

We might also fear that after a while we will forget our child, what they looked like, sounded like, smelled like and that if we should dare to have a little fun and start to enjoy life again, we would be papering over those memories, or that by 'softening' the pain of our grief we would somehow be assisting the passage of our child's death to the mists of time. We know these fears well. We remember our own anxiety about Joshua's death becoming more commonplace 'as he takes his place in the shared anonymity of all the worlds dead', something Jimmy wrote about in his book of photos and poems *Released* – published a mere six months after Josh died.

If there's a barometer of pain, we know that even after eleven years the anguish of grief still registers high in our psyches. But what we've discovered and what we'd like to share with you and anyone who may not be as far into their bereavement, is that a proactive approach to grief, especially the process of creating new images and stories that belong in the 'now', liberating memories from the past and rejuvenating them in ways that they become embedded in our lives today… this is where healing occurs. The scars will always be there, but we can be comfortable and accepting of their presence – they need not deter us from living life to the full again.

ten things we have learned

When Josh died, we moved from one world into another. From a known and certain world to one where previous ambitions and assumptions about what we wanted from life were thrown into total confusion. In the eleven years since Josh's death, we have found (in common with many other bereaved parents) a kind of invisible barrier has come between us and those who have not experienced the death of one of their children. This is nobody's fault. This is the way it is. And clearly, we would not wish this grief on anyone. Grief is painful, and emotionally and physically exhausting. It is also very confusing. In our Western world, bereavement and how to deal with difficult feelings are not things we are accustomed to acknowledging.

Hopefully the following ten observations will help to bring a little more understanding. We offer these from our own perspective, but they should apply to bereavement of any kind.

1 You can't fix our grief

Our grief is not an illness, nor is it just some unfortunate thing getting in the way of a 'normal, happy life.' Our grief is here to stay. Our child has died, but that doesn't mean that we stop loving them or that they are not present in our lives anymore. Grief is the form love takes when someone dies and our grief is important to us – it is how we are learning to live inside our loss, how we carry what cannot be fixed. In a strange way we need our grief – it is how we survive.

So please don't do or say anything that you think will make it go away. To do so is to reduce further what is already a broken heart.

2 There is no timetable for grief

People say that time is a healer, but the grief we have for our child has no end. This grief is for life. It's not something we will 'get over'. What you may observe is that grief comes in waves – at times overwhelming, at times barely noticeable, but it will never go away.

Please don't judge or make assumptions about how long we should grieve. And don't ever ask a bereaved parent to move on or find closure. It's for us to decide how we get on with life and platitudes about what our child would want are just not helpful.

3 Grief for a child is not like other kinds of grief

When a parent or a grandparent dies, it is in the natural order of things. Death comes to us all, but the death of a son or daughter (of whatever age) is out of tune with nature. The death of a child is never a natural event and is always in the wrong order of things. For most bereaved parents, life will now seem very unfair. Consequently, our grief is going to be of a different order. This is not to say that other forms of grief aren't valid, just that the death of a child can produce a number of more complicated responses. When an older person dies, generally speaking we have a whole life story to remember – we have their history to tell. When a child dies it's not only their history, it's their future we have also lost.

4 Know that we have changed

Bereaved parents are very different people from who we were before our child died. If you haven't recognised that, then know that it is true. When our child died a

huge part of us died too. Well, that's what it feels like and in our attempts to reconstruct our lives again, to find a purpose to carry on, many previous assumptions will be challenged and we will be discovering many new insights that will have a profound effect on who we are. We have been traumatised by our child's death and the shock to the system has provoked a new way of looking at life. Our priorities may have changed, our views about faith and the afterlife may have changed, and we are in the process of finding ourselves again in what has for us become a very uncertain world.

Please have patience while we learn how to trust again. If our response to your offers of help seem ungrateful, please believe that this isn't personal. Our culture offers us very few examples of how to grieve openly, fully and purposefully, and we may well act in ways that are not becoming to the person you thought you knew.

5 Don't be afraid to talk about my child or to say their name

We will not crumble or cry at the mention of our child's name. And even if we do it's not you that has caused our tears. In any case, these will more likely be tears of joy that you have decided to share a memory with us. These tears are actually a kind of release in the same way that laughter is. Our child's death has left a huge hole in our lives (and maybe in yours, too). More than anything we want to talk about our child, to remember how s/he lived even more perhaps than how s/he died. To recall memories with you is to know that you cared for our child and that you care for us. But perhaps more than that, sharing stories about our child's life will help us to accept their death – to make it more real. Our greatest fear is when everyone stops talking about her or him, as if s/he never existed. Remembering to include their name on Christmas cards is always a good thing.

6 Much of the time we will hide our grief

Bereaved parents are very good at putting on a mask – and the longer it's been since our child died, the better we become at hiding our grief. When you meet us, we may laugh and joke, but that could well be a cover for what's really going on. Our lives may appear normal but often we are really struggling just to get out of bed in the morning. We wish we weren't so broken, for the pretence can be physically and emotionally exhausting. Grief is exhausting and it's not something we necessarily want to share. That might be difficult to understand, but sometimes it's like we are living in a parallel universe and it's not one we would want you to join.

There will also be times when we will need to hold the pain of our loss so close to our hearts that any attempt to relieve it will be rebuffed. These are very private, almost sacred moments, and they are not to be shared – save perhaps with others who are similarly bereaved.

Please try not to be offended if you feel shut out from our grief – this is not personal.

7 Don't run away from our grief

Grief is frightening. We get that. And grief following the death of child is even more frightening. It's frightening for you and it's frightening for us. We have been told that we, and our situation, are every parent's worst nightmare. So, we understand how difficult it can be to connect with us, with our grief and with our new reality. It is also really confusing, and contrary to the previous request we do ask you not to run away from our grief. If you've tried calling and get no answer, send an email or text message. Let us know that you are always there so that when the time is right we can call you back.

When we do talk about how we are doing, try just to listen and to accept what are some very strong emotions. Remember, there is nothing you can do to bring our child back. Similarly, there's nothing you can do to fix our grief. We know how painful, how awkward and how helpless this could make you feel, but if you can hold on to those feelings and stay with us, silently if necessary, but always without judgement, then we will know how much you really do care.

8 Think before you speak

Oh yes, this is so important. Many of you will not know what to say when you meet a bereaved parent. This is to be expected – and it is absolutely ok to admit that. Finding the words to describe our loss is hard for us too. In a way, it's better to remain silent than come out with

inane platitudes. Frankly, our child might not be 'in a better place', and it matters not that we may have other children to care for. Neither are we about to start making another one as a replacement. We know you mean well, but please don't say you understand unless you really do. We don't need you to interpret our grief or to advise us of a better way to grieve.

9 Do some research on child loss and parental grief

This will help enormously should you want to find out more about parental bereavement. There is no rule book for how to grieve after the death of a child, but some general knowledge of the subject will help engage with and support us with more empathy. (Note: empathy, not sympathy.)

There is a wealth of literature available on how bereaved parents adapt and survive after the death of a child. In the United Kingdom, The Compassionate Friends is a good resource. In the United States there is a wonderful website: Refuge in Grief, which, while not specific to child loss, is good for an understanding of the day-to-day concerns of the bereaved.

Of particular interest for us is the concept of continuing bonds and our efforts to maintain a meaningful relationship with the deceased. We believe this is a healthier approach to grief, supplanting as it does older ideas about 'finding closure' or 'moving on'.

10 Grief can be a period of growth – there are benefits to be had from grieving

Grief is not all doom and gloom. There is much to be learned from our grief, but perhaps more from the grief that other parents will experience after the death of a child.

We all suffer – at some point in our lives we will all face tragedy and turmoil of one kind or another. Some would say that the only true connection between two human beings is through suffering. It's not through joy or good times. The real heart-to-heart connection is through suffering and discomfort. And it's then that we can see change in ourselves and growth in our understanding of others. Because if you are not hurting, if you are not uncomfortable, then there is no impetus for change. Why change what's not broken? Bereaved parents have been broken and inevitably that forces us to look at life anew and to change – mostly, we think, for the better.

acknowledgements

We'd like to thank all the contributors to this book, many of whom we have met only since and because our son died. Their openness and honesty in telling of their grief have encouraged us immensely and we owe them a deep debt of gratitude for sharing their stories, for their varied and unique insights to the complexities of their own responses to loss and for helping us develop our own understanding of the way creativity and a proactive approach to grief benefits us all.

For their astute observations on earlier drafts to make this a volume we are so proud of, we are indebted to Dr Janet Richardson, Ollie Huddleston and Helen Hunt for their forensic attention to detail, to Dr Kathryn Mannix for her own wisdom and lessons in curiosity, and Prof Robert Neimeyer for making the time. Their foresights and encouragement have mattered more than they will ever know. We'd also like to thank Fran Landsman for her interpretation of the Conrad novel pictured on the frontispiece.

Much of what we have learnt and have shared here is the result of our engagement with many other bereaved parents and siblings who have joined us on our Active Grief Weekends and we'd like to show our appreciation to them and the core TGGP team, Jo Bousfield for her joy in the written word and continually inspiring us to follow her lead, Gill Mann for simplifying and bringing a more sensitive approach to our photography workshops, to Sharon Jackson for quieting our souls and showing us how to breathe, and to Lizzie Pickering who for many years has been a beacon of love, light and laughter and a constant source of wisdom when it comes to a proactive grief.

The Good Grief Project is a family affair and for their commitment and enthusiasm, Joshua's brother and sister Joe and Rosa deserve a special mention. Not only have they endured the pain of Josh's death and the continuing heartache of his absence as bereaved siblings, they have also had to negotiate their way round their parents' grief. They have done this with much love and sensitivity and we in turn love them for it. Their own contribution to our Active Grief programme continues to be outstanding. Joe for his dedication to helping others explore the physical impact of grief and Rosa for providing the delicious meals that inevitably led to those more relaxed but significant conversations in which our guests share their grief.

We are especially grateful to Jannet and Stephen Mathers who following the death of their own daughter Jessica in 2007 founded The Jessica Mathers Trust to support several different charities including The Good Grief Project. Their help over the past decade has been invaluable both in establishing the project and in maintaining a secure financial base for it to grow. Without their backing this book would not exist.

In the background but not unnoticed are the trustees and volunteers of The Good Grief Project – our chair Andy Freedman (always a source of true friendship and encouragement), Jo Bousfield (again a mine of creative ideas), Tom Kilh (without whom we would not be able to connect with our online community), Sara Tibbets (for her gentle wisdom and cinematic expertise) and Annabel Richmond who has so enthusiastically embraced our cause and sustained our presence on social media.

We now give massive thanks to Katy Bevan of Quickthorn whose belief in our ideas and the importance of sharing them is the starting point for this book. Her encouragement, understanding and patience as she guided us through the production process has been invaluable.

Thank you, Katy, for giving us this opportunity and for holding the reins so sensitively.

Does it go without saying that we give thanks to Joshua? This is a difficult one. We would of course prefer this not to be the case, but without his death (but more crucially his life) none of this would be happening. No films, no charity, no book, and no real understanding of the universal experience of suffering and loss. We'd like to think but hate to admit we are better people for it. So just as there's no forgetting, there's no end of gratitude or our love for our boy.

Finally, a word of appreciation to you, dear reader. Whether you are bereaved or not, whether your grief is recent or more mature, whether you give 'professional' advice or friendly support, you have crossed a line and been unafraid to enter a room full of difficult, often painful, but always amazing conversations that in many small ways reveal much that is essential to our common humanity – love, resilience, and gratitude.

bibliography

References to books and articles quoted in the text.

Page 16 Weller, Francis, *The Wild Edge of Sorrow: Rituals of Renewal and the Sacred Work of Grief,* North Atlantic Books (2015)

Page 20 Charde, Sharon, https://www.sharoncharde.com/

Page 20 Whitehead, Gregory, *Four Trees Down from Ponte Sisto,* https://gregorywhitehead.net/2012/10/27/four-trees-down-from-ponte-sisto/

Page 22 Rodman, Fiona, *Sifting for Gold – Mourning and Transformation,* University of Middlesex (2011)

Page 30 Leader, Darien, *The New Black: Mourning Melancholia and Depression,* Penguin (2009)

Page 41 Pierce, Sophie, *The Green Hill: Letters to a Son,* Unbound (2023)

Page 46 Harris Edmonds, Rosa, *Making it Real – Death and Photography,* Beyond Goodbye website

Page 54 Bray, Simon, *Loved&Lost,* self-published (ongoing)

Page 60 Edmonds, Jimmy, *Released,* self-published, Blurb (2011)

Page 83 Andrews, Gary, *Finding Joy,* John Murray (2020)

Page 94 Carmody Nathan, Jessica, *My Jupiter,* Young Poet Records (2022)

Page 102 Whyte, David, *The Well of Grief,* from River Flow: New & Selected Poems, Many Rivers Press (2012)

Page 106 & 114 Oliver, Billie, Blog, https://justkeepswimmingbillie.wordpress.com/

Page 107 Nichols, Wallace J, Blue Mind: How Water Makes You Happier, More Connected and Better at What You Do, Abacus (2018)

Page 107 Huttunen, P., Kokko, L. & Ylijukuri, V., Winter swimming improves general well-being, International Journal of Circumpolar Health (2004)

Page 110 Fitzmaurice,Ruth, *I Found My Tribe,* Penguin Vintage (2017)

Page 117 Frankl, Viktor, *Man's Search for Meaning,* Beacon Press (1945)

further reading

Too many to mention and this is far from a complete list, but we've found the following books and articles enlightening in one way or another.

Bates, Sasha, *Languages of Loss: A psychotherapist's journey through grief,* Yellow Kite (2020/2021)

Bowlby, John, *Attachment and Loss – Trilogy,* Pimlico (1997)

Brown, Brené, *Daring Greatly,* Penguin Life (2015)

Cacciatore, Joanne, *Bearing the Unbearable: Love, Loss and the Heartbreaking Path of Grief,* Wisdom (2017)

Clarke, Rachel, *Your Life in My Hands: A Junior Doctor's Story,* Metro Books (2017), *Dear Life: A doctor's story of love and loss,* Little, Brown (2020), *Breathtaking: Inside the NHS in a Time of Pandemic,* Little, Brown (2021)

Crossley, Diana and Kate Sheppard, *Muddles, Puddles and Sunshine,* Hawthorn Press (2014)

Devine, Megan, *It's OK that you're not OK: Meeting Grief and Loss in a Culture That Doesn't Understand,* Sounds True (2017)

Didion, Joan, *The Year of Magical Thinking,* Harper Perennial (2006)

Freud, Sigmund, *On Murder, Mourning and Melancholia,* Penguin Classics (2005)

Gawande, Atul, *Being Mortal: Illness, Medicine and What Matters in the End,* Profile Books (2015)

Harris, Jane with Jimmy Edmonds, *Exploring Grief with Photography,* Bereavement Care, Taylor and Frances Online (2015)

Kessler, David, *Finding Meaning: the sixth stage of grief,* Scribner (2019)

Klass, Dennis, with Silverman and Nickman, *Continuing Bonds: New Understandings of Grief,* Routledge Taylor and Francis (1996)

Kübler-Ross, Elisabeth with David Kessler, *On Grief and Grieving: Finding the Meaning of Grief through the Five Stages of Loss,* Simon & Shuster UK, Reissue (2014)

Lewis, C.S, *A Grief Observed,* Faber & Faber (1961)

Mannix, Dr Kathryn, *With The End In Mind* and *Listen,* Harper Collins (2019/2)

Pickering, Lizzie, *When Grief Equals Love,* Unbound (2023)

Rosen, Michael, *The Sad Book,* Walker Books (2011)

Samuel, Julia, *Every Family has a Story*, Penguin (2022)

Shepherd, Alison, *Opening the door to Grief,* The British Medical Journal (2018)

Stroebe, Margaret with Henk Schut, *The Dual Process Model of Coping with Bereavement,* Taylor & Frances online (2010)

Thompson, B.E. & Neimeyer, R.A. (Eds) *Grief and the Expressive Arts: Practices for Creating Meaning*, New York Routledge (2014)

Van der Kolk, Bessel, *The Body Keeps the Score: Mind, Brain and Body in the Transformation of Trauma,* Penguin (2015)

Williams, Mark with Danny Penman, *Mindfulness : A Practical Guide to Finding Peace in a Frantic World,* Generic (2011)

Worden, William, *Grief Counselling and Grief Therapy* (5th edition 2022)

resources

A far from comprehensive list of organisations and networks that you might find helpful when looking for more information and support.

The Good Grief Project – thegoodgriefproject.co.uk Our own charity offering support to bereaved parents and siblings

At a Loss – www.ataloss.org Signposting to bereavement support

British Association for Counselling and Psychotherapy – www.bacp.co.uk Professional association for members of the counselling professions in the UK

Child Bereavement UK – www.childbereavementuk. org Support for children and adults

Children with Cancer UK – www.childrenwithcancer. org.uk Leading national children's charity dedicated to the fight against cancer

The Compassionate Friends – www.tcf.org.uk Peer-to-peer support for bereaved parents and siblings

Cruse Bereavement Support – www.cruse.org.uk Support, advice and information

The Good Grief Trust – www.thegoodgrieftrust.org Signposting to bereavement support

Hospice UK – www.hospiceuk.org (leading palliative care and end of life charity) Dying Matters – www.

hospiceuk.org/our–campaigns/dying–matters Campaign arm of Hospice UK

The Lullaby Trust – www.lullabytrust.org.uk Support following the death of a baby or young child

Marie Curie – www.mariecurie.org.uk Care and support through terminal illness

Meningitis Now – www.meningitisnow.org Support for people with meningitis

Mind – www.mind.org.uk Mental health advice and support

National Bereavement Alliance – nationalbereavementalliance.org.uk Support for those working with the bereaved

Now I Lay me Down to Sleep (NILMDTS) – www. nowilaymedowntosleep.org US based photography agency producing remembrance portraits for those experiencing the death of a baby

The Outdoor Swimming Society – www. outdoorswimmingsociety.com UK based but international organisation promoting wild swimming of all kinds

Papyrus – www.papyrus-uk.org Prevention of young suicide

Samaritans – www.samaritans.org 24 hours 365 days helpline

Shapes of Grief – www.shapesofgrief.com Grief training for those who grieve and those who support them

Sudep Action – sudep.org Research, education and support for families following a sudden and unexpected death from epilepsy

Survivors of Bereavement by Suicide – uksobs.org Support for those grieving after a suicide

Together for Short Lives – www.togetherforshortlives. org.uk Supporting families of children with life-limiting conditions

UK Council for Psychotherapy – www.psychotherapy. org.uk Register for psychotherapists and psychotherapeutic counsellors in the UK

Winston's Wish – www.winstonswish.org Child bereavement support services for families and professionals

What's Your Grief – whatsyourgrief.com US based online resource

In the years since their son's death Jane and Jimmy have produced a number of documentaries including *Beyond Goodbye* (about Josh's funeral), *Gerry's Legacy* for Alzheimer's Society, *Say Their Name* for The Compassionate Friends, the award winning *A Love That Never Dies* and *Beyond the Mask* (about the experience of grief during Covid).

Keep up to date with their work by visiting @thegoodgriefproject, on Instagram and Facebook and @goodgriefproj on Twitter, or their website: www.thegoodgriefproject.co.uk

When Words are Not Enough © 2022 Jane Harris and Jimmy Edmonds
Jane Harris and Jimmy Edmonds are hereby identified as the authors of this work in accordance with section 77 of the Copyright, Designs and Patent Act, 1988. They assert and give notice of their moral right under this Act.

Published by Quickthorn
Elm Cottage, Dark Lane, Chalford GL6 8QD
E-mail: info@quickthornbooks.com
Website: www.quickthornbooks.com

All rights reserved. No part of this book may be reproduced, stored in a retrieval system or transmitted in any form by any means (electronic or mechanical, through reprography, digital transmission, recording or otherwise) without prior written permission of the publisher.

Mindful of our impact on the environment, Quickthorn uses ethically sourced materials, local suppliers and printers in the UK.

Editor: Katy Bevan
Photography by Jimmy Edmonds
Design and typesetting by Chris J Bailey © 2022
Printed in the UK by Cambrian Printers
Printed on environmentally friendly chlorine-free paper sourced from renewable forest stock

David Whyte, *The Well of Grief*, printed with permission, © Many Rivers Press, Langley, WA, USA

British Library Cataloging in Publication Data applied for
ISBN 978-1-912480-57-9